my revision notes

CCEA GCSE

ENGLISH LANGUAGE

Amanda Barr

HODDER
EDUCATION
AN HACHETTE UK COMPANY

The publisher would like to thank the following for permission to reproduce copyright material:

Acknowledgements:

p. 26: Jan Moir: from 'Uniform wars: it's the parents who need a dressing down', http://www.dailymail.co.uk/news/article-3780880/JAN-MOIR-Uniform-wars-s-parents-need-dressing-down.html (*Daily Mail*, 9 September 2016) © MailOnline; **p. 35: Emma Sophina:** from 'Experience: I crash-landed in the Hudson', https://www.theguardian.com/lifeandstyle/2012/aug/17/experience-i-crash-landed-in-hudson (*Guardian*, 17 August 2012), copyright Guardian News & Media Ltd 2017; **p. 36: Ernest Shackleton:** from *South: The Story of Shackleton's Last Exhibition* (Macmillan, 1919), public domain; **p. 37: Siegfried Sassoon:** from 'A soldier's declaration' (July 1917) copyright Siegfried Sassoon by kind permission of the Estate of George Sassoon; **pp. 46–47: HSE (Health and Safety Executive):** from www.hse.gov.uk/pubns/indg337.pdf, reproduced under the Open Government Licence v3.0 (www.nationalarchives.gov.uk/doc/open-government-licence/version/3/); **p. 54: Fermanagh Lakelands:** www.fermanaghlakelands.com/Portals/0/downloads/FLTHistoryTrail.pdf; **p. 63: Charles Dickens:** from *Oliver Twist* (1838, Richard Bentley), public domain; **p. 67: Evelyn Waugh:** from *Brideshead Revisited* (1945, Chapman & Hall), reproduced under fair usage; **pp. 68–69: Susan Hill:** from *The Woman in Black* (1983, Vintage), reproduced under fair usage; **p. 71: George Eliot:** from *The Mill on the Floss* (1860, William Blackwood), public domain; **pp. 73–74: Maya Angelou:** from *I Know Why the Caged Bird Sings* (1869, Virago) published by Little, Brown Books and used with permission; **p. 74: H.G. Wells:** from 'The Red Room' (1896, *The Idler Magazine*), public domain; **p. 77: Charles Dickens:** from *Great Expectations* (1864, Chapman & Hall), public domain; **p. 81: Theresa Breslin:** from *Whispers in the Graveyards* (1994, Egmont), text copyright © 1994 Theresa Breslin, published by Egmont UK Limited and used with permission; **p. 82: Gary Paulsen:** from *Hatchett* (Simon and Schuster, 1987), reproduced by permission of Flannery Literary © Gary Paulsen; **p. 86–87: Oliver Smith:** from '21 reasons why I hate museums', http://www.telegraph.co.uk/travel/lists/21-reasons-why-I-hate-museums/ (*The Telegraph*, 19 August 2014), © Telegraph Media Group Limited 2017; **p. 87: Anna Hart:** from 'Generation selfie: has posing, pouting and posting turned us all into narcissists?', http://www.telegraph.co.uk/women/womens-life/11265022/Selfie-obsession-are-we-the-most-narcissistic-generation-ever.html (*The Telegraph*, 5 December 2014), © Telegraph Media Group Limited 2017.

Photo credits:

p. 49 tl © Getty Images/iStockphoto/Thinkstock; **p. 49 tr** © Shutterstock/mimagephotography; **p. 49 br** © michelaubryphoto – Fotolia; **p. 49 bl** © Ilike – Fotolia.com; **p. 50 tl** © .shock – Fotolia; **p. 50 tr** © ANGEL MANUEL FERNÁNDEZ – Fotolia.com; **p. 50 c** © Anton Gvozdikov – Fotolia.com; **p. 50 b** © Mariusz Prusaczyk/123RF.com; **p. 51 t** © Nick Biemans – Fotolia; **p. 51 b** © Privilege – Fotolia; **p. 52 b** © .shock – Fotolia; **p. 56** © volff – Fotolia; **p. 66** © JackF – Fotolia; **p. 68** © SVLuma – Fotolia; **p. 69** © tallyclick/123RF.com; **p. 75** © fred goldstein/Fotolia.com

Orders: please contact Hachette UK Distribution, Hely Hutchinson Centre, Milton Road, Didcot, Oxfordshire, OX11 7HH. Telephone: +44 (0)1235 827827. Email education@hachette.co.uk. Lines are open from 9 a.m. to 5 p.m., Monday to Friday. You can also order through our website: www.hoddereducation.co.uk

© Amanda Barr 2018

First published in 2018 by
Hodder Education
An Hachette UK Company,
Carmelite House, 50 Victoria Embankment
London EC4Y 0LS

Impression number 7

Year 2022

Cover photo © ragnarocks/123RF

Illustrations by Integra Software Services Pvt. Ltd., Pondicherry, India

Typeset in Bembo Std Regular 11/13 by Integra Software Services Pvt. Ltd., Pondicherry, India

Printed by Ashford Colour Press Ltd.

ISBN 9781471888618

Get the most from this book

Everyone has to decide his or her own revision strategy, but it is essential to review your work, learn it and test your understanding. These Revision Notes will help you to do that in a planned way, topic by topic. Use this book as the cornerstone of your revision and don't hesitate to write in it – personalise your notes and check your progress by ticking off each section as you revise.

Tick to track your progress

Use the revision planner on pages 4, 5 and 6 to plan your revision, topic by topic. Tick each box when you have:

- revised and understood a topic
- tested yourself
- practised the exam questions and gone online to check your answers and complete the quick quizzes

You can also keep track of your revision by ticking off each topic heading in the book. You may find it helpful to add your own notes as you work through each topic.

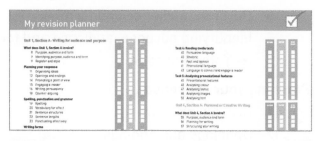

Features to help you succeed

My revision planner

REVISED   TESTED   EXAM READY

REVISED   TESTED   EXAM READY

Unit 4, Section B: Reading literary and non-fiction texts

What does Unit 4, Section B involve?

Test yourself answers

Countdown to my exams

6–8 weeks to go

- Start by looking at the specification — make sure you know exactly what material you need to revise and the style of the examination. Use the revision planner on pages , 5 and 6 to familiarise yourself with the topics.
- Organise your notes, making sure you have covered everything on the specification. The revision planner will help you to group your notes into topics.
- Work out a realistic revision plan that will allow you time for relaxation. Set aside days and times for all the subjects that you need to study, and stick to your timetable.
- Set yourself sensible targets. Break your revision down into focused sessions of around 40 minutes, divided by breaks. These Revision Notes organise the basic facts into short, memorable sections to make revising easier.

REVISED ☐

2–6 weeks to go

- Read through the relevant sections of this book and refer to the exam tips, how to prepare for the exam, typical mistakes and key terms. Tick off the topics as you feel confident about them. Highlight those topics you find difficult and look at them again in detail.
- Test your understanding of each topic by working through the 'Test yourself' questions in the book. Look up the answers at the back of the book.
- Make a note of any problem areas as you revise, and ask your teacher to go over these in class.
- Look at past papers. They are one of the best ways to revise and practise your exam skills. Write or prepare planned answers to the exam practice questions provided in this book.
- Track your progress using the revision planner and give yourself a reward when you have achieved your target.

REVISED ☐

One week to go

- Try to fit in at least one more timed practice of an entire past paper and seek feedback from your teacher, comparing your work closely with the mark scheme.
- Check the revision planner to make sure you haven't missed out any topics. Brush up on any areas of difficulty by talking them over with a friend or getting help from your teacher.
- Attend any revision classes put on by your teacher. Remember, he or she is an expert at preparing people for examinations.

REVISED ☐

The day before the examination

- Flick through these Revision Notes for useful reminders, for example the exam tips, how to prepare for the exam, typical mistakes and key terms.
- Check the time and place of your examination.
- Make sure you have everything you need — extra pens and pencils, tissues, a watch, bottled water, sweets.
- Allow some time to relax and have an early night to ensure you are fresh and alert for the examinations.

REVISED ☐

My exams

GCSE English Language Unit 1

Date:...

Time:...

Location:..

GCSE English Language Unit 4

Date:...

Time:...

Location:..

What does Unit 1, Section A involve?

What is being assessed?

Section A is assessing your writing skills. This means you are being assessed on the quality and accuracy of your written work.

What will you have to write?

You will be given a topic to write about and will be expected to promote a point of view and persuade your audience to agree with you. The question will identify the topic for discussion, the audience you are writing for and the form your writing should take.

How long do you have?

You have 55 minutes in which to complete one task. It is advised that you spend up to 15 minutes planning for writing, 30 minutes writing your response and 10 minutes checking over and editing your work.

How many marks are available?

The total number of marks available in Section A is 87. Up to 57 marks are available for producing an organised and interesting piece of writing which matches form with purpose to engage the interest of a reader. Up to 30 marks are available for using a range of sentence structures and accurate spelling, punctuation and grammar.

How much are you expected to write?

Whilst it is expected that you will produce an extended response, you should prioritise the quality of your writing, rather than focusing on delivering a set quantity of writing. You should ensure there is a clear introduction, development and conclusion and, as this task requires you to promote a point of view, you will do that successfully when your ideas are developed and confidently expressed.

Purpose, audience and form

REVISED

When promoting a point of view, you are effectively demonstrating your ability to argue and persuade. As well as writing for a specific purpose, you will be writing for a given audience (for example, teenagers or parents) and may be tasked to write in a particular form (for example, a speech or an article).

The examiner is looking for a response that:
- writes with relevance about the set topic
- shows understanding of the **purpose** of the writing
- reads like an article, speech, blog or whatever **form** is stated
- writes in a way that is appropriate for the intended **audience**.

> **purpose**: why the text has been produced
>
> **form**: how the text has been constructed and structured
>
> **audience**: who the text is for – the reader

Identifying purpose, audience and form

REVISED

The task itself will identify:
- the topic you are writing about
- why you are writing (purpose)
- who you are writing for (audience)
- how you should write (form).

For example:

1 Write a speech (a) to be delivered to your classmates (b) to persuade (c) them of the benefits of reading (d).
- (a) Form
- (b) Audience
- (c) Purpose
- (d) Topic

2 'Modern sports stars are overrated and overpaid.' (a) Write an article (b) for your school magazine (c) in which you share your views on this topic (d).
- (a) Topic
- (b) Form
- (c) Audience
- (d) Purpose

> **Exam tip**
>
> Blogs take different forms and many can be written using **colloquial** English. Remember, in an exam you should use Standard English as you are writing for an examiner.

Tasks

Identify the topic, purpose, audience and form in each of these tasks:

1 Write a letter to your local council to persuade them to invest more money in leisure facilities in your area.

2 Write a blog in which you promote your views on whether the legal driving age should be increased to 21.

3 Write an article to be published in your local newspaper to persuade young people to get involved in volunteer work.

> **colloquial**: conversational and informal

Test yourself

TESTED

Read the opening paragraph to a student's response and complete the tasks which follow:

1 Compose the exam question to accompany this student response. You should identify topic, purpose, audience and form.

2 Write down three things you would advise this student to do to improve their response.

3 Rewrite this response so the content is suitably matched to purpose, audience and form.

> Right everyone, listen up, I am talking now and I want you to listen. Today I want to talk to you about school uniform and why I think it needs to be scrapped. Do you agree or not? I think it is really ugly and really uncomfortable. Everything about this uniform is ugly, the material, the colour and the style. And it costs a fortune. I really hate having to put this ugly outfit on five days a week.

Answers on p. 88

Register and style

REVISED

It is important to use the correct tone and register in your response. For example, you would be more formal when writing to your head teacher than you would when writing for your peers. However, never forget that, in an exam situation, the examiner is your primary audience. For this reason, avoid being too informal and never use slang.

Tasks

Rank these writing tasks in order of formality, beginning with the most formal and working down to the least formal:

1 A letter to an MP to persuade them to visit your school.
2 A speech to your classmates to share your views on the benefits of after-school clubs.
3 An article for your school magazine to persuade the school community to become eco-friendlier.
4 An email to a friend to persuade them to go to the cinema at the weekend.
5 An online blog presenting your views on the benefits of social media.

Test yourself

TESTED

Select one of the above tasks and write a short opening paragraph which shows your appreciation of audience, purpose and form and adopts an appropriate register and tone.

Answers on p. 88

Planning your response

You will have 55 minutes to complete Section A. It is advised that the first 15 minutes are spent planning your answer. There are two parts to the planning process:

1 Generating the ideas you will use in your writing.
2 Organising your ideas and selecting a structure.

The examiner is looking for a response that:
- develops logically
- moves confidently and **coherently** from one paragraph to another
- avoids unnecessary repetition of ideas
- includes a variety of **linguistic devices** to engage the reader
- employs a variety of sentence types and sentence lengths.

Organising ideas

REVISED

When planning, many students adopt the following approach:

1 Locate and highlight key words in the question.
2 Record ideas in a spider diagram or bullet-point list.
3 Develop each idea by noting down key points to make and/or techniques to use.
4 Decide the best order to write ideas and how they can be linked, then number them.

Tasks

1 Highlight the key words in this task:
Write an article (a) for publication in an educational magazine (b) in which you present your views (c) on the topic: 'We should all be forced to learn a foreign language at school.' (d)
  (a) Form
  (b) Audience
  (c) Purpose
  (d) Topic
2 Now record your ideas in a planning diagram:

We should all be forced to learn a foreign language at school.

It's far too difficult.

It's not necessary for a successful career.

3 Add two more ideas to the planning diagram above.
4 Develop each idea; for example:

---

coherently: in a logical way

linguistic devices: specific techniques which are used to achieve an effect such as: alliteration; rhetorical questions; hyperbole and repetition, to name a few

Exam tip

If you have a plan you will feel more confident about being able to write an extended response; you will not forget to include important points and, as you write, you can concentrate on *how* you express your ideas.

Exam tip

A plan will look untidy as you are recording ideas as they come to mind. Don't write in full sentences when planning.

Exam tip

To ensure you can produce an extended response, you will need to think of five or six ideas which you can develop into detailed and interesting paragraphs.

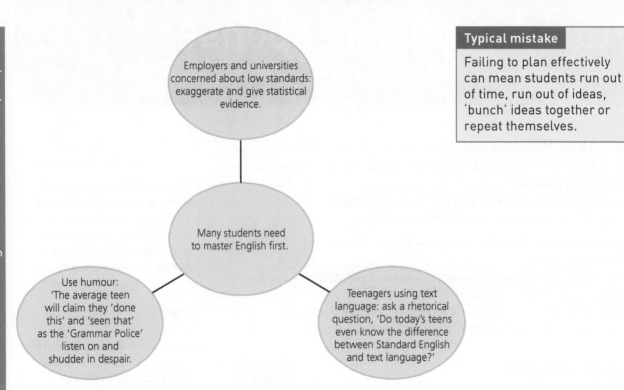

5 Decide the order in which you will present your ideas.

Test yourself

Complete the full planning process for this Unit 1, Section A task: Write an article for your school website persuading readers that it is stressful to be a teenager in today's world.

Answers on p. 88

Openings and endings

It is important to open strongly as this is where the examiner forms their first impression of you as a writer. Remember, examiners mark a lot of scripts so they appreciate a response which is original and hooks and holds their attention. Your introduction should show an awareness of audience, purpose and form. For example, think about how the opening of a speech would differ from the opening of an article.

There are a variety of ways to engage your reader by using linguistic devices, such as a rhetorical question or a personal anecdote, but you can also vary your sentence structures and use punctuation to enhance meaning.

Below are two introductions in which students give their opinions on the use of mobile phones in school:

Student A

I think mobile phones should be allowed in school. I bring my mobile phone to school every day and I know lots of other pupils do the same. There are lots of reasons why mobile phones should be allowed in schools and I will share some of them with you.

Student B

> Are we really ready to relax the ban on mobile phones in school? Stop for a minute and consider the consequences: pupil concentration will certainly suffer; teacher stress will increase; cyber-bullying will soar and exam results will plummet! School is definitely not the place for a sophisticated and expensive piece of kit such as the modern smartphone...

Tasks

1 Devise a list of success criteria which would help Student A to write a better introduction.

When concluding your response, you want to leave a lasting impression upon your reader. The conclusion is not the place to introduce anything new, instead you should try to appeal to the minds and hearts of your audience and compel them to share your point of view.

2 Below is the conclusion written by Student B. As you read it, highlight what the student has done well:

> Undoubtedly, technology has enhanced our life in many ways and most teenagers suffer separation anxiety when their mobile phone is not to hand, but it is hard to see a compelling reason for introducing mobile phones into our classrooms. As much as I hate to admit it, we teens are simply not disciplined enough to get through the day without tallying up our 'likes', keeping up to date with our newsfeeds and indulging our selfie obsession. After all, few of us actually use our phone to make phone calls, and guess what? If an emergency were to occur, the school office has its very own retro landline! Do yourself and all your peers a favour, leave the phone at home ... grades depend on it.

You should have spotted the student used:

- ○ inclusive language: 'our', 'we' and 'us'
- ○ humour/exaggeration: 'suffer separation anxiety' and 'retro landline'
- ○ triple: 'without tallying up our "likes", keeping up to date with our newsfeeds and indulging our selfie obsession'
- ○ connectives to link ideas: 'After all'
- ○ a question to engage the reader: ' ...and guess what?'
- ○ **imperatives:** 'Do yourself a favour, leave...'
- ○ exclamatory sentences, ellipsis and inverted commas.

> **Assessment comment**
>
> This is a Level 5 response as the student confidently uses language to leave an impression upon the reader. They successfully connect with their reader and write in an engaging and lively style.

> **Imperative:** an order or command

Mark scheme

Read the mark scheme below and identify what you need to do to achieve the higher levels.

Level 1	Limited awareness of audience and purpose.
	Uncomplicated style with simple/few language techniques.
	Limited evidence of structural features.
Level 2	Some awareness of audience and purpose.
	Ideas are developed to promote a point of view or compel the reader.
	Some recognition of form.
	Some successful attempts to use language techniques and structural features.

Level 3	Clear awareness of audience and purpose.
	Ideas are developed in an interesting way with a range of language techniques to engage or compel the reader.
	Writes with a clear appreciation of form.
	Evidence of a variety of structural features.
Level 4	Confident awareness of audience and purpose.
	Ideas are developed in a way that is increasingly convincing and compelling.
	Confident recognition of form.
	Successfully uses a variety of language techniques throughout the response with structural features used to enhance meaning and/or engagement.
Level 5	Highly impressive awareness of audience and purpose.
	Highly confident development of a range of ideas to make the piece engaging and interesting.
	Assured recognition of form.
	Highly confident in using a full range of language techniques to achieve effects.
	Assured organisation of ideas with structural features.

Test yourself

TESTED

Plan in detail and then write the opening and concluding paragraphs for this task: Write a speech in which you persuade your audience to recycle more and be less wasteful.

Aim to:
- complete your detailed plan in 15 minutes, including identifying the techniques you will use in each paragraph to engage your reader
- produce an interesting introduction and conclusion which uses linguistic devices, varies sentence lengths and uses punctuation to enhance meaning.

Answers on p. 88

Promoting a point of view

REVISED

When you promote your point of view, you want your audience to be convinced by what you say and share your opinions. To do this successfully, you should use a range of persuasive techniques which will help you put forward a convincing argument which appeals to the heart and mind of your reader. You will want to establish a positive **rapport** with your reader, which means you will acknowledge the reader throughout your response.

> **rapport**: a positive connection or relationship

The examiner is looking for a response which:
- confidently and convincingly develops ideas
- uses a range of linguistic devices which help engage a reader
- positively connects with the reader.

You will not convince anyone to share your opinions unless you can develop your reasoning. Remember, you will not make an argument in one or two sentences.

> **Typical mistake**
>
> Students often prioritise communicating their opinions on a given topic and do not give enough thought to *how* they are writing so that they interest their reader.

Tasks

1 Read these two extracts written by GCSE students trying to persuade their audience to be more charitable. Decide which one is more successful in promoting their point of view:

Student A

> You just never know when you might find yourself needing help from others. Life can be unpredictable and no man is an island. For this reason, I strongly believe that we should all be a little more charitable.

Student B

> Being charitable is not about being wealthy, it's about being human. To be frank, we have all become increasingly selfish but this benefits nobody! As one person, you might not be able to end world hunger but you can make a difference in the lives of others through small acts of kindness such as giving up your seat on the bus or train, smiling more and even lifting litter to help create a cleaner environment for us all. These actions cost nothing but if we all introduced them into our everyday interactions, wouldn't the world be a better place? Wouldn't we feel better about ourselves?

2 Improve the response written by Student A by developing the ideas so that they are more clear and convincing.

Engaging a reader

The most important thing to do to engage your reader is to believe in what you write. Your reader will be swayed by writing which is passionate and convincing. Having hooked the reader's attention in your opening paragraph, you must work to maintain their interest throughout your writing. You can do this by:

- using a range of persuasive techniques to appeal to the heart and mind of the reader (these are explored in more detail on page 16)
- using a variety of sentence structures to make your writing lively (these are explored in more detail on page 21)
- using conversational phrases to 'talk' to your reader.

Whilst you do not want to be too informal, you should address your reader directly:

I know what you're thinking...	Let me tell you...	Can you believe...?	You may have heard...
...shocking, I know.	For what it's worth...	Like me, you will...	We all know...
To be frank...	It wouldn't be an overstatement to say...	Just take a minute to reflect upon that...	How many times have you...

Task

Read the extract below taken from a student's response to the task: Write a speech where you discuss the educational benefits of school trips.

Decide what could be included at the relevant points, to make the response more engaging.

...**A**... school trips are nothing more than a day out of school. ...**B**... I truly believe that they are a valuable opportunity to bring learning to life. ...**C**... heard young people ask, 'Why are we learning this?' Young people need to appreciate the relevance of their learning, they need to understand how classroom content connects to the real world. ...**D**... school trips are probably one of the most effective and memorable learning opportunities a young person can experience.

Test yourself

TESTED

Write a paragraph where you argue that school trips are too expensive and do not offer value for money. Include three phrases to engage your reader.

Answers on p. 88

Writing persuasively

REVISED

You will have encountered a range of linguistic devices throughout your study of English at Key Stages 3 and 4. You may have devised an acronym to help you remember the most common techniques. The important thing is to show you can skilfully use a range of persuasive techniques throughout your response.

Remember, you begin by generating your ideas first and then plan how to work the various techniques into your writing to enhance the delivery of your ideas. You must also express yourself confidently, even disguising your opinion as fact to make your writing convincing.

> **Exam tip**
>
> Many students use this acronym to help them remember persuasive techniques:
> - **R** Repetition
> - **A** Alliteration
> - **I** Imperative
> - **N** Name an expert
> - **F** Facts
> - **O** Opinions
> - **R** Rhetorical questions
> - **E** Emotive language
> - **S** Statistics
> - **T** Triple/rule of three

Tasks

1 Practise using a range of persuasive techniques by rewriting the sentences below to make them more persuasive:
   (a) Completing homework is important if you want to do well in school.
   (b) Too many young people are not getting enough exercise.
   (c) I think we are too reliant on technology.
   (d) Computer games are fun.
   (e) If you sponsor a pet you can give it a better life.
2 Rewrite each of three paragraphs below, making them more persuasive by including the persuasive techniques listed:

First attempt	Rewrite to include...	Redraft
Modern sports stars are grossly overpaid. Not only do they take home a large salary for the little work they do, they also earn a lot of money from sponsorship deals.	Rhetorical question Statistics	
We consume too much junk food. We know the risks that come with eating such an unhealthy diet, but we just can't seem to stop. We are setting ourselves up for a whole range of health problems.	Exaggeration List of three Name an expert	

First attempt	Rewrite to include...	Redraft
We should all be taught first aid in schools. This is a valuable skill. By teaching first aid in schools we would be creating a safer, less selfish society. Life is precious and there is no reason why people should suffer or even die because we were too lazy to learn basic first aid. First aid saves lives.	Repetition Imperative Emotive language	

3 Read the extract below from a student's response to the following task:
  Write a speech for your classmates persuading them of the benefits of part-time work.
  Then answer the prompt questions.

There is nothing more rewarding than earning your own money and being able to indulge yourself at the end of the working week. No more must I endure the humiliation of begging my parents for a loan, only to be forced to clean the entire house in return for a few paltry pounds. No more must I miss out on epic adventures with friends due to an empty purse. No more must I save for months to be able to afford the latest 'must-have' purchase. I can have it all! Did you know that, on average, UK parents spend a whopping £520.00 per month per teenager? Not in my house!

What's more, a part-time job doesn't just offer financial freedom, it provides you with something much better, something so precious it is desired by employers the length and breadth of the country. I am of course speaking of ... experience! As we all know, it's a fiercely competitive world out there. According to Professor Kelly from Queen's University Belfast, 'Employers are no longer simply seeking qualifications, they want to see more, they want to see young people gaining experience either in a paid or voluntary capacity.' Heed this advice, a part-time job shows your ability to manage a demanding workload, it proves you have ambition and it equips you with the confidence to interact with people. Do yourself a favour, get a part-time job. You won't regret it.

How is the writer's opinion presented persuasively in this opening sentence?

What words are employed effectively in this sentence?

What is the writer's intention in using repetition of 'No more...'?

Explain how this sentence is effective in engaging a reader.

Identify three techniques used in this sentence and explain their impact upon a reader.

How is the writer effective in engaging the reader here?

Explain the impact of the imperative statement here.

What technique is the writer employing here and to what effect?

Explain how this short sentence persuades the reader.

Assessment comment

This is a strong Level 5 response which shows evidence of using language for effect. The student is making choices about their use of language in order to make their writing interesting and convincing. They successfully connect with their audience.

Test yourself

TESTED

Plan in detail and write the opening and concluding paragraphs for this task: Write a speech which you will deliver to your class to persuade them of the benefits of homework.

Remember to:
- spend 10–15 minutes producing a detailed plan which includes your ideas and the techniques you will use
- engage your reader by using a variety of techniques and well-chosen words and phrases.

Answers on pp. 88–89

Counter-arguing

REVISED

As well as promoting your point of view on a given topic, you should also show an ability to counter-argue. To effectively counter-argue, you should think about the ways in which your audience might disagree with you – acknowledge their point of view and then point out why they are wrong.

Tasks

Read the extract below taken from a student's response to the task: Write an article where you present your views on raising the school leaving age to 18.

> Whilst I am an advocate of raising the school leaving age to 18, I am aware of others who argue that an increase would simply cost too much money as schools' expenses would soar. However, this argument is weak as we must not put a price on what is best for our young people and our society. Think about the number of sixteen-year-old school leavers who are unemployed and cost the state money to re-educate and re-train once they realise how few opportunities actually exist in today's society. The fact is, that keeping young people in school will almost certainly reduce unemployment levels and produce a more educated workforce.

1 Identify in the extract above where the student:
  ○ demonstrates an awareness of opposition
  ○ begins their counter-argument
  ○ closes the argument.
2 Practise writing a suitable counter-argument to follow these statements:
  (a) I am a firm supporter of the National Lottery and the impressive amount of money it raises for good causes, however I know critics will argue it encourages gambling…
  (b) I am addicted to reality television! Of course my opponents will claim it is deceptive and cruel but…

Exam tip

To develop your argument, you can use phrases such as:
- furthermore…
- moreover…
- in addition…

To introduce counter-arguments you can use:
- however…
- on the other hand…
- on the contrary…
- but…

Test yourself

TESTED

Write an article in which you put forward your views on the topic: 'The internet is addictive and dangerous.'

Plan in detail and write two paragraphs where you promote your opinion in an engaging style, acknowledge your opposition and put forward a convincing counter-argument.

Answers on p. 89

Spelling, punctuation and grammar

Given that up to 30 marks are available for spelling, punctuation and grammar, you must give attention to writing accurately, employing a variety of sentence structures and employing a widening vocabulary.

The examiner wants to see a response in which:
- basic spelling, punctuation and grammar are accurate
- there is a deliberate attempt to use more sophisticated vocabulary for effect
- a range of sentence types and sentence structures have been used
- there is a deliberate attempt to use more ambitious punctuation to enhance meaning.

Spelling

You will not have access to a dictionary in the examination but this should not hinder you from attempting more ambitious vocabulary. GCSE students know words they commonly misspell and you should take steps to correct habitual errors.

The following words are often misspelt by students:

a lot	accidentally	successful
believe	perform	definitely
difference	embarrass	environment
especially	excitement	argument
outrageous	form/from	committee
humour/ humorous	information	interesting
receive	maybe	necessary
dilemma	disappoint	opportunity
surely	truly	professional

> **Exam tip**
>
> You want to impress your examiner, so take risks with your vocabulary. It is much more impressive to see a student attempt to use ambitious vocabulary and not quite get the spelling correct, than to read a response in which the student plays it 'safe' by using simple and uncomplex vocabulary which they can spell.

Tasks

1 Think of five words you regularly misspell and devise a way of remembering the correct spelling.

2 Make sure you know when to use the following words correctly:

to/too/two	are/our	affect/effect
their/there/they're	chose/choose	principal/principle
of/off	threw/through	quite/quiet
your/you're	where/were/we're	right/write
now/know/no	practise/practice	lose/loose

Test yourself

Read the following response. Identify and correct the ten spelling errors:

Learning to play a musicle instrument is very benefical as it helps to manege stress and is an excellent stress reliefer. Everyone should have the oppurtunity to learn to play an instrument. Research shows that listening to music and playing an instrument can stimulite the brain and improve your memory. When you play you must concentrate and playing with others is espshially effective as you must listen closely to the harmonies. Learning to play an instrument requires alot of practise and you will learn how to manage your time affectively.

Answers on p. 89

Vocabulary for effect

Showing you can use a wide and varied vocabulary will improve your writing and allow you to express yourself with increasing sophistication. In preparation for your exam, compile a word bank of vocabulary which you find impressive and will aim to use in your writing.

Tasks

1 Using a thesaurus, find two **synonyms** and two **antonyms** for each of the following words:
   ○ bad
   ○ walked
   ○ lovely
   ○ said
   ○ happy

> **synonym**: a word which is similar in meaning to another word
>
> **antonym**: a word which is opposite in meaning to another word

> **Exam tip**
>
> Remember, there is a spectrum of emotions so be precise with your vocabulary; being concerned is not the same as being alarmed. Being afraid is not the same as being petrified. Feeling elated means more than feeling content. Your word choices matter!

2 In each of the sentences below, substitute the word(s) in bold with a more precise choice of word or phrase:
   (a) I **love** growing up in the twenty-first century!
   (b) I feel **unhappy** when I hear people say, 'Young people have it so easy.'
   (c) Ask any young person and they will admit that school **is not good**.
   (d) The internet has **changed** our world for the better.
   (e) I was **delighted** to discover that most sixteen year olds **want** to vote.

You should also be choosing vocabulary for effect. For example, think of the differences between these two statements:

A If we do not limit our consumption of junk food we are facing an obesity **problem**.

B If we do not limit our consumption of junk food we are facing an obesity **crisis**.

The word 'crisis' is more emotive and more effective in getting the reader to feel concern. Decide whether you want your reader to think/

feel positively or negatively, as this will influence your language choices and help you control the reader's response. For example, if you support street art you might describe it as: 'a creative form of self-expression'. The adjective 'creative' makes your claim more positive. If you oppose street art you might describe it as: 'an ugly eyesore'. The adjective 'ugly' strengthens your critical tone.

3 Select a suitable word(s) to complete each of these statements:

(a) Fox hunting is…

(b) Forcing young people to do homework, after six … hours of school is…

(c) Examinations are…

(d) Testing cosmetics on … animals is…

Test yourself

TESTED

Write two paragraphs promoting your views on the topic: 'Animal testing is unnecessary and cruel'.

Remember to:
- write convincingly
- use a variety of techniques to add interest and engage your reader
- make deliberate decisions about vocabulary to influence how your reader thinks and feels as they read your response.

Answers on p. 89

Sentence structures

REVISED

How you write is as important as what you write. You can enhance your content by writing in a way that is confident and lively. Using a variety of sentence types and sentence lengths shows you are a confident writer and are writing to hold the interest of your reader.

Your response should include the following:
- **Simple sentences** – these communicate one idea and contain one verb. For example, 'It is important to eat healthily.'
- **Compound sentences** – these are a series of simple sentences joined together using a simple connective such as 'and', 'but' or 'so'. They have two or more verbs and communicate more than one idea. For example, 'It is important to eat healthily and look after your body.'
- **Complex sentences** – like compound sentences, these have two or more verbs and communicate more than one idea. However, one part of the sentence is subordinate to the other, which means it does not make sense on its own. For example, 'It is important to eat healthily and look after your body by following a balanced diet and participating in regular exercise.'

Task

Read the extract below and identify one simple sentence, two compound sentences and one complex sentence:

Going to university no longer increases your career prospects, improves your living standards or rewards your ambition with a desirable salary, instead it burdens you with crippling debt. University tuition fees are unfair! Tuition fees must be abolished as they are a tax on learning. Tuition fees punish the poor and they benefit the wealthiest.

> **Exam tip**
>
> Try to include different sentence types in each of your paragraphs. This is something you can look for when you read over and check your work.

Sentence lengths

As well as using a variety of sentence types, you should also vary your sentence lengths. A good piece of music will have 'rises' and 'falls' which give it a rhythm. Similarly, you want your writing to flow in a way that holds the attention of your reader.

Tasks

1 Up to 30 marks are available for spelling, punctuation and grammar, including using a variety of sentence structures. Study this student-friendly mark scheme to identify what you need to do to achieve the top levels.

Mark scheme

Level 1	Simple sentence structuring.
	Basic punctuation used with some accuracy.
	Limited vocabulary with some accuracy in spelling of simple words.
Level 2	Straightforward sentence structuring.
	Accurate use of simple punctuation, such as full stops and commas, to achieve straightforward communication.
	Some evidence of vocabulary used to enhance the response with accurate spelling of uncomplicated words.
Level 3	Some variation in sentence structures.
	Accurate use of full stops, commas, question marks and exclamation marks with some evidence of punctuation used to add impact.
	Attempts to use a wide and varied vocabulary with accurate spelling of straightforward words and some more complex words.
Level 4	Deliberate variation in sentence structures.
	Employs a range of punctuation throughout the response to maintain precision in expression and engage the audience.
	Evidence of a precise and varied vocabulary with only occasional errors in the use of challenging words.
Level 5	A full range of sentence structures are used.
	Confidently uses a full range of punctuation.
	Evidence of sophisticated vocabulary and virtually all spelling is accurate.

2 Read both extracts below from two different responses to the task:
Write an article in which you present your views on corruption in sport.
Decide which student varies their sentence structure more effectively.

Student A

Sport is full of corruption. We can't continue to claim otherwise. There are lots of examples to prove this fact. There are reports of footballers betting on games. There are athletes taking performance-enhancing drugs. There are even coaches who will force their 'star' to break the rules in order to win.

Student B

Let's be blunt – modern sports is corrupt! It seems that not a week goes by without another breaking sports scandal. No longer is sport about taking part; it's all about the win and it seems our 'stars' are prepared to go to any lengths to emerge victorious. How much longer can we continue to applaud our Olympians? It seems personal bests and world records are being broken on a daily basis and I can't help but question the validity of these record-breaking performances. It all seems a little too super-human. Who is really to blame though? For me personally, corruption reached a whole new level of unsavoury when we discovered that coaches were actually encouraging and facilitating cheating in a desperate desire to claim gold. I simply cannot fathom why an individual would put their professional reputation on the line in this way. It's indefensible!

Test yourself

TESTED

Write a paragraph in which you defend sport and modern-day sports stars.

Remember to engage your reader by:
- using a variety of sentence types and sentence lengths
- using a variety of linguistic devices
- carefully choosing your vocabulary.

Answers on p. 90

Punctuating effectively

REVISED

It is important to punctuate accurately but you will also be rewarded for using a range of punctuation which shows you can go beyond basic full stops, capital letters and commas. You should demonstrate an ability to use punctuation to enhance your writing.

Using basic punctuation

Take note of how this student uses punctuation:

Do we really want corporal punishment back in our schools? I think not! Corporal punishment is not the solution to improving classroom discipline. Young people, who want to learn, will feel intimidated and fearful. Mr Tom Kelly, Principal of Hartswood College, agrees as he claims, 'School should be a nurturing environment where young people feel safe and are free to make mistakes. We simply can't condone physical punishment. No civilised society would even consider reintroducing corporal punishment.'

> **Exam tip**
>
> Do not overuse the exclamation mark or it will lose impact.

> **Typical mistake**
>
> Students frequently fail to make full use of punctuation to enhance meaning.

Like this student, you will be expected to use:
- capital letters to begin sentences and for proper nouns
- an appropriate end-stop at the end of a sentence – a full stop, question mark or exclamation mark
- commas to separate additional information within a sentence and to introduce direct speech within a sentence
- apostrophes to indicate omission or ownership

- speech marks around the words spoken. Note that punctuation such as full stops are placed inside the closing speech marks.

Task

Write a short, seven-sentence paragraph where you agree or disagree that tattoos and piercings are unattractive. Ensure you correctly use capital letters, end-stops, commas, apostrophes and speech marks.

Using more ambitious punctuation

- A **colon** follows a general statement and introduces a list; for example, 'John ate the same things every lunchtime: a chicken sandwich, a packet of crisps and an apple.'
- A **semi-colon** separates items in a list; for example, 'John left the shop with a bag full of treats: a king-sized chocolate bar; two large packets of his favourite crisps; a two-litre bottle of cola, which was on offer; a packet of jellies and some chewing gum.'
- A **semi-colon** can also be used in place of a full stop to connect two closely related sentences; for example, 'It was pitch black inside the house; I was petrified.' Here the character feels petrified because of the darkness inside the house so the semi-colon makes clear the connection.
- **Brackets** can be used to share additional information with your reader. Think of them as a way of introducing aside comments; for example, 'Mr Sharpe (Head of Year 11) will address the students at their next assembly.'
- **Dashes** are used to add an informal thought into a sentence; for example, 'Homework is incredibly important – not to mention boring – so we must stop complaining and get on with it.'
- **Ellipses** suggest there is more to come and can be used effectively to intrigue your reader; for example, 'Just think about the risks that come with spending hours in front of a screen…'

> **Exam tip**
>
> Apostrophes for omission are needed when two words have been joined together. The apostrophe is placed where letters have been omitted; this is not always where the two words join:
> - Do + not = don't.
> - Apostrophes show ownership.
> - Singular noun? Add 's'; for example, 'The boy's book.'
> - Plural noun ending in 's'? Just add an apostrophe after the 's'; for example, 'The boys' books.'
> - Plural noun that doesn't end in 's'? Add an apostrophe and 's'; for example, 'The children's books.'

Task

Write a short seven-sentence paragraph where you promote the benefits of travelling. Ensure you use basic punctuation accurately and include three examples of more ambitious punctuation to enhance your writing.

Test yourself

TESTED

Write three paragraphs in which you promote the benefits of introducing financial education to the school curriculum. You should:
- make accurate use of basic punctuation
- include at least four examples of more ambitious punctuation.

Answers on p. 90

Writing forms

Speeches

REVISED

Throughout your GCSE course you will have opportunities to deliver speeches as part of Unit 2 (Speaking and Listening) so you will appreciate that all successful speeches begin in written form. When writing a speech, you will want to:

- acknowledge your audience quickly to hook their interest
- establish a positive rapport and hold their interest throughout your speech
- be convincing and interesting – make your audience believe in you and what you are saying.

Remember, speeches are written to be heard so as well as making sure your content is interesting, you will need to ensure ideas are well organised.

Tasks

1 Read the short extract below which was taken from a GCSE student's response to the task: Write a speech to be delivered to your school principal to persuade him/her that your year group deserve a school trip.

> Dear Principal,
>
> I have been asked to talk to you and tell you why my year group deserve a school trip. I think we deserve a school trip because we have worked hard all year and are on track to secure good results which will reflect well on the school. A trip could be a learning opportunity. School is not just about exam results so a trip would be good for us and help us create memories we will never forget.

This student has not been very successful in engaging the attention of their audience and they fail to establish a positive rapport. Whilst their ideas are valid, they are not expressed in a convincing or interesting style. Rewrite the opening passage to make it more engaging and interesting so that you hold the attention of your audience.

2 The extract below has been taken from a student's response to the task: Write a speech to be delivered to Year 8 students to persuade them to stay safe online.

> Good morning Year 8 students, allow me to begin by asking you to raise your hand if you have a social media account. As expected, I can see that most of us in the room are regularly online and enjoying the benefits of social media. Like you, I too am tempted by the wonders of the online world but have you ever wondered how safe we really are online? As an older student, I have probably been tweeting and Snapchatting more than most of you. I've always regarded myself as someone who is sensible and aware of how to keep safe in both the real world and the virtual world. Let me share with you a recent experience which taught me a lesson in the importance of e-safety...

Highlight the above response to indicate where the student has been successful in engaging their audience and establishing a positive rapport.

Test yourself

Write a speech to be delivered to your local council to persuade them to organise a festival for young people.

Answers on pp. 90–91

Articles

In an exam situation you should not worry about achieving the appearance of an article, so do not attempt to write in columns or include images and captions. You can, however, include a heading or title, and you may wish to add in sub-headings but these are not essential; getting the content and tone right is what matters.

Task

Read the extract below, which has been taken from a newspaper article published in the *Daily Mail*. Answer the prompt questions to help you appreciate how the writer promotes his views in an interesting and engaging style:

Uniform Wars

Day Four and the siege of Hartsdown Academy continues. On one side, new headmaster Matthew Tate who wants to raise standards by insisting that all pupils come to school correctly attired in their uniforms. No deviations, please. No trendy shoes, short skirts, trainers, overt jewellery, novelty knots in ties and general scruffiness. On the other side, belligerent parents who object to what they see as a heavy-handed approach and are refusing to cooperate with the strict policy.

On Day One, 50 pupils at his Kent school were sent home for being incorrectly dressed. On Day Two, amid increasing uproar, another 20 were told to go home and get dressed properly. Many parents were livid. Tempers flared and voices were raised at the gates as teachers were accused of 'ruining' the little darlings' first day at school. Pupils wept as mums and dads opted to stand and argue instead of accepting the new rules — or, perhaps, going to the school outfitters to make amends.

I have to say, if anyone was setting a bad example, it was the mums and dads. And I don't care if the new rules were complicated or open to interpretation. It's their responsibility to get their kids to school, on time, in the right gear. And railing against authority when they fail to do so helps no one, least of all themselves.

How does the heading hook the reader's interest in the article?

How does this abrupt opening help to engage the reader in the story?

What does this list tell the reader about the standards set by the new headmaster?

What impression of the parents does the writer convey through the adjective 'belligerent'?

What does this background information and statistics add to the story?

How does this short sentence succeed in holding the reader's interest?

Why has the writer waited until now to openly declare his opinion?

How does this final sentence encourage us to agree with the writer?

You can see in the above example that the writer is not primarily concerned with reporting the facts but also shares his opinion and influences the reader's impression of this story. The facts alone would make for an uninteresting read!

Also note how the writer has structured his article:
- He begins by introducing the main thread of the story – a conflict between parents and a new headteacher.
- The writer cannot assume the reader has previous knowledge of this story so he contextualises it by providing background details including facts – 'On Day One…', 'On Day Two…'
- He includes descriptive details so the reader can visualise the scene at the school gates – 'voices were raised … pupils wept…'
- He declares his personal opinion on the whole affair – ' …if anyone was setting a bad example…'

Plan and write a short article for your local paper in which you promote your concerns about the increasing number of fast-food outlets in the neighbourhood. Remember to engage and interest your reader. Think carefully about how you will structure your writing.

Answers on pp. 90–91

Letters

REVISED

Formal letters traditionally look like this:

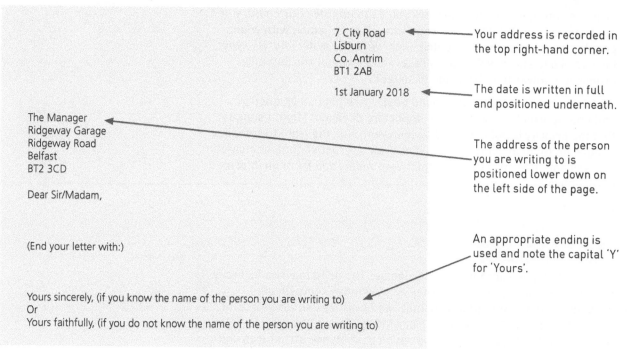

7 City Road
Lisburn
Co. Antrim
BT1 2AB
— Your address is recorded in the top right-hand corner.

1st January 2018
— The date is written in full and positioned underneath.

The Manager
Ridgeway Garage
Ridgeway Road
Belfast
BT2 3CD
— The address of the person you are writing to is positioned lower down on the left side of the page.

Dear Sir/Madam,

(End your letter with:)
— An appropriate ending is used and note the capital 'Y' for 'Yours'.

Yours sincerely, (if you know the name of the person you are writing to)
Or
Yours faithfully, (if you do not know the name of the person you are writing to)

Letters usually begin with an introduction which outlines the reason for writing. They will then go on to develop and give finer details before ending with a paragraph outlining what the sender hopes will happen next.

> **Exam tip**
>
> Avoid beginning a letter with 'I am writing to...'

Task

Compare the opening paragraphs to the two letters below. Both are written to a politician to offer views on allowing sixteen year olds the right to vote:

Student A

> Dear Paul, I am writing to let you know that your policy to give sixteen year olds the right to vote is a load of rubbish. I'm seriously scundered that you and your party actually think anyone with half a braincell will back you on this. I mean, how many sixteen year olds do you know who have the first clue about politics? Most of them can't decide what they wanna eat for dinner. I say, get real mate, it ain't gonna happen...

> **Assessment comment**
>
> Student A shows awareness of audience and purpose. They attempt to engage their audience through direct address and asking questions but they do not write using the correct register and it is too informal. Their spelling is mostly accurate but their vocabulary is uncomplicated and punctuation is accurate but limited. This is a Level 2 response.

Student B

> Dear Minister,
>
> I wish to commend you for the work you do to improve our country and am especially grateful for your commitment to engaging with young people and recognising the contribution we make to society. However, I would like to share with you my reservations about the current proposal to lower the voting age to sixteen.
>
> My first concern is that many young people are politically ignorant, and unprepared to make such an important decision. Might I suggest that the priority is not to extend sixteen year olds the right to vote, but to educate them in politics and cultivate an interest so that, at eighteen years of age, they may exercise their vote wisely and from an informed perspective ...
>
> Furthermore...

> **Assessment comment**
>
> Student B begins appropriately, recognises the need to write formally and achieves the correct tone. They employ more sophisticated vocabulary and avoid colloquialisms. See how they use less forceful language to promote their opinion by stating, 'Might I suggest...' This is a Level 5 response. Improved variation in sentence structures and increased variation in punctuation would move it into the upper end of this level.

Test yourself

TESTED

Plan and write a letter of your own to your local tourist board about the need for improved tourist attractions in Northern Ireland.

Answers on pp. 90–91

Online blogs

REVISED

The word 'blog' comes from 'web-log', which is an online diary. Blogging has become popular as people share their views and experiences with the online community. Blogs are usually 'chatty' in style and written using the first person. Of course, anything that is posted online has the potential to reach a wide and varied audience so again there is a need to make the writing interesting and engaging.

Blogs often include images and weblinks but there is no need to include these features in an exam where it is the content that counts.

Task

Read this extract taken from an online blog:

Shopping Hell

Confession time – I hate shopping! There, I've said it. I should have said it long before now because for the last six hours I have trudged the city centre, pretending to be excited by finding the 'perfect' shoes to match an extortionately priced and impractical handbag. I struggled to contain my horror as my girlfriends would squeal in delight as they made their way to the changing rooms caressing dresses and blouses. (I swear their high-pitched squeals are certain to have sent nearby dogs into a barking frenzy.) For me, there's only one way to shop and that is online!

You can see that the writer shares their experience of shopping by using humour and exaggeration to hold the interest of the reader. They also use a variety of sentence lengths to hold the reader's interest. Punctuation such as brackets helps achieve the chatty and conversational style whilst the exclamation mark emphasises the writer's strong feelings.

The writer continues their blog by discussing the advantages that online shopping has over the high-street experience. Write the next paragraph of the blog, describing the experience of shopping online and emphasising how it is a more pleasant experience.

Test yourself

TESTED

Plan and write an online blog where you promote your views on television talent shows. Remember you must appeal to a wide and varied audience so use a range of techniques to engage their interest.

Answers on pp. 90–91

How to prepare for the exam

Reading and writing go together. To improve your writing, you should read as widely as you can. In preparation for Unit 1, Section A, read articles in newspapers, online and in magazines where the writer is promoting a point of view. As you read, underline or highlight how the writer uses language and structural features for effect.

Recognise how Unit 2 (Speaking and Listening) can help you prepare for Unit 1, Section B by engaging in class debates and discussions. Try giving a presentation to your class where you strongly promote your point of view; for example, 'The three changes I would make to school/education/twenty-first-century living' or 'Why Xbox is better than PlayStation'. Choose your own topics or ask your teacher to give you some practice writing tasks. The more practice you have in promoting your opinion, the more confident you will become.

Take every opportunity to practise your writing skills by writing for different audiences and in different forms. Review all tasks which your teacher has marked so you can identify your strengths and weaknesses.

What does Unit 1, Section B involve?

What is being assessed?

Section B is assessing your reading skills. This means there are no marks available for spelling, punctuation and grammar, but it is important that you express yourself clearly and confidently so the examiner can understand your ideas and reward your efforts.

How long do you have?

You have 50 minutes in which to answer four tasks (Tasks 2–5 on the examination paper). Two tasks are based on your reading of a non-fiction text and two are based on a media text. Each task will state how long you should spend answering and it is important that you follow this advice.

How many marks are available?

The total number of marks available in Section B is 63.

What will the questions ask?

There are four tasks to complete in Section B (Tasks 2–5).

Task 2	21 marks	15 mins	You will have to read an extract from a non-fiction text and analyse how the writer presents ideas.
Task 3	12 marks	10 mins	You will have to read an extract from a non-fiction text and show understanding by identifying two pieces of information which you summarise and explain using your own words. Each explanation should be supported by two pieces of relevant textual evidence.
Task 4	20 marks	17 mins	You will read an extract from a media text and analyse how the language influences a reader.
Task 5	10 marks	8 mins	You will study a section taken from a media text, select two presentational features and explain how they influence a reader.

Exam tip

The text extracts to accompany Tasks 2 and 3 are taken from the same text. Tasks 4 and 5 are also based on the same text.

Identifying purpose

REVISED

You should be clear about the purpose of the text. The language and presentational features will be selected by the writer to help them achieve their purpose.

Exam tip

Remember, a text can have more than one purpose!

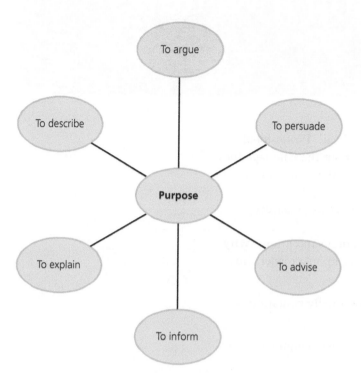

Task

Read the statements below and identify their purpose:

Statement	Purpose?
Don't miss out on this limited offer! Buy today for blemish-free skin.	
Don't bottle up your concerns, share them with someone you can trust.	
It is completely wrong to claim that young people are over-worked.	
Dog owners spend an average of £586.44 per year on their pet.	
Young people are feeling under increasing pressure because social media tells them they must look, act or think a certain way to gain acceptance or 'likes'. They can't escape the constant scrutiny and judgement of the online world.	
Imagine waking up every morning to a spectacular sunrise, a breath-taking vista of palm trees and a cloudless blue sky.	

Task 2: Analysing a writer's craft

To **analyse** means to examine something in close detail. Professional writers craft their texts, making careful decisions about the language they use and the impression it will have upon a reader. In the exam you should be able to:

(a) identify **what** decisions have been made by the writer regarding language and presentational features

(b) provide an explanation which considers the writer's intentions (**why** he/she employs certain features) and the impact upon a reader (**how** the reader responds).

Exam questions which require you to analyse will usually contain the word 'how', such as:

Explain how the writer conveys the experience of the camping trip in a way that engages the reader.

OR

Analyse how the writer conveys his memories of travelling to Donegal as a child.

OR

Consider how the writer has succeeded in creating an interesting piece which engages the reader.

Timing

You will have 15 minutes to complete Task 2 and there are 21 marks available.

What is the examiner looking for?

The examiner wants to see that you can:

- read and understand texts – both **explicit** and **implied meaning**
- select relevant evidence
- analyse by commenting on how a writer's use of words and phrases, language techniques and structural features influence a reader.

> **explicit meaning:** meaning which is clearly stated by the writer
>
> **implicit meaning:** meaning which is suggested but not directly stated by the writer

> **Exam tip**
>
> Remember, in Section B of the exam *you* are the reader of the text extracts so consider how you think and feel as you read through them. Try to select words, phrases and techniques which leave an impression upon you.

Point. Evidence. Explain. (P.E.E.)

REVISED

Many students find P.E.E. useful when responding to texts.

- P: Make a point about the text.
- E: Quote evidence from the text.
- E: Explain the effect upon a reader.

Tasks

1 Read the extract below from a student's response. Mark 'P' where the student makes a point, mark 'Evid' where they provide supporting evidence and 'Exp' where they begin to explain.

> The writer uses lots of positive adjectives in the text. Words such as 'luxurious', 'spectacular' and 'unforgettable' are used. The writer uses these words to make the reader form a positive impression about the hotel. They make the reader think that the accommodation is sophisticated and somewhere they will enjoy staying. The reader thinks that a stay here would be worthwhile as the owners have gone to a lot of effort to impress their customers and make their stay comfortable and memorable.

2 Read this extract below from a restaurant review. As you read identify words and phrases used to convey the writer's negative experience of visiting the restaurant. Practise responding by writing one P.E.E. paragraph.

> The décor was dated and unimpressive. The carpet was a ghastly shade of green and even the dim lighting failed to conceal the stomach-churning stains dotted across it. We should have turned and left but before we had the chance, a surly waiter plonked us at a table and thrust a few menus in front of us before slouching off to join his colleagues who were slumping around the bar area.

3 Read the following extract that was published in *The Telegraph* and read the sample responses on page 34, which answer the task:
Explain how the writer emphasises the unpleasant nature of his journey.

> After a few minutes aboard the coach, the glitz and glamour of the cruise ship seemed a million miles away. Each village we passed through seemed less impressive and more derelict than the one before. Eventually, we came to a stop in a small grey town. A long line of traffic snaked before us, each car covered in a thick grey dust and spewing out thick grey fumes. Our shiny white tour bus looked completely out of place as it lumbered along the pot-hole-riddled road.
>
> The town looked like a relic from an ancient past; it was a crumbling grey concrete jungle and I found myself longing to return to our majestic boat and sail away across turquoise waters. Sensing our unease, the coach driver thought it would be a good idea to distract us. Excitedly, he pointed to the remains of an army tank, ravaged by rust and sitting in the grounds of an ancient building, like some grotesque memorial to Croatia's troubled past. I never discovered the actual name of this place, but I chose to name it 'Ghost Town'.

Mark scheme

The marks awarded for Task 3 are levelled, which means the examiner will compare your response against the level descriptors and decide where your answer best fits.

Look at the student-friendly version of the mark scheme below, and then read the sample responses and the level awarded for each:

Level 1	A simple attempt to offer some basic comments on the writer's craft. May offer some selection of relevant evidence.
Level 2	A straightforward response which identifies some language choices and/or language techniques with some attempt to select relevant evidence and offer a limited explanation.
Level 3	A more detailed consideration of the writer's craft with generally accurate selection of evidence followed by an appropriate explanation.
Level 4	Begins to analyse the impact of a range of words and phrases, language devices and structural features. Will offer an accurate and convincing explanation based on a range of mostly accurate evidence.
Level 5	A highly confident analysis which considers words and phrases, language devices and structural features. Will select a range of accurate evidence followed by a detailed and confident explanation which will zoom in on specific language uses.

Student A

The writer makes his journey seem unpleasant when he states the road was 'pot-hole-riddled'. This means there were a lot of pot-holes. It also says the houses were 'crumbling' and the cars were 'spewing out thick grey fumes'.

Assessment comment

This response offers basic comments. They select relevant evidence but do not offer any explanation. This is a Level 1 response.

Student B

The writer makes his journey seem unpleasant by stating how the sights got 'less impressive and more derelict'. With this phrase, the writer emphasises to the reader how the sights got more unappealing and concerning as the bus journey continued. The writer makes us think that he does not feel at ease as words and phrases such as 'snaked,' 'crumbling', 'grey dust' and 'relic' force the reader to think of death, decay and danger which make the experience seem unpleasant and tense. The writer does not make it seem like a place you can relax and have an enjoyable holiday. He states that he gave it the name 'Ghost Town' as there were no signs of life here.

Assessment comment

This is a more detailed response with generally accurate selection of evidence, considering technique (repetition) and words and phrases. The explanation is appropriate. This is a Level 3 response.

Student C

From the beginning of the passage the writer makes his journey seem unpleasant by implying the coach trip transported him to a different world, away from the ostentatious setting of the cruise ship. He describes feeling like he was 'a million miles away' from the ship's 'glitz and glamour', suggesting the villages were characterised by poverty and felt isolated. He states,'Eventually, we came to a stop in a small grey town.' The adverb 'eventually' forces us to **infer** the journey has been long and unpleasant and the adjective 'grey' suggests the place is unimpressive, ugly even. It is clear that the town fails to make a positive first impression as the writer comments on the traffic jam which 'snaked before us' with cars 'spewing out thick grey fumes' making the reader conjure up an unpleasant image of congestion and pollution. The verb 'spewing' and the repetition of 'grey' make the place seem repulsive and help us understand the writer's fervent desire to return to the beauty and tranquillity of 'turquoise waters'. The road is 'pot-hole-riddled', with 'riddled' making the holes seem excessive. Here the writer reinforces a negative impression of the town itself, depicting it as a neglected place which has suffered from a lack of investment.

infer: to read between the lines – to arrive at a reasoned conclusion based on what is suggested or implied

Assessment comment

Student C's response offers a confident analysis and considers the impact of language upon a reader. The student zooms in on specific words and can comment on structural features such as how the writer communicates the unexpected nature of his encounter with the town. They also show a confident ability to infer and select relevant supporting evidence. This is a Level 5 response.

4 Write two more paragraphs to complete the analysis of the Croatia text above. Use the mark scheme to decide which level best describes your response.

Test yourself

TESTED

Read the extract below and answer the task:

The writer of this piece is recalling when her plane crash landed in the Hudson River. Explain how the writer emphasises the sense of drama to engage the reader.

Moments later the captain made an announcement: 'This is the captain, brace for impact.' I had to figure out how to brace myself because, of course, I had never paid attention to the emergency drill. In the end, I grabbed the seat in front and held on tightly. Just in time. The impact came with incredible force – I'm still amazed I walked away without any injuries. As we landed tail first, we were hurled back into our seats, then plunged forwards. Someone screamed, 'We're in water.' We all jumped to our feet, jostling towards the exit doors.

By now, water was rising as the back of the plane was submerged. I could hear people screaming and one instinct took over: I need to get out. By the time I reached the exit door, freezing water was up to my shins. I could see passengers standing outside on the icy wing. Aware of others behind me, I jumped into one of the life rafts. I was soaking and shivering, from the water as well as the wind howling down the river.

From www.theguardian.com/lifeandstyle/2012/aug/17/experience-i-crash-landed-in-hudson

Answers on p. 91

How to prepare for the exam

You will need to practise your analysing skills.

1 Read plenty of non-fiction extracts from newspapers, travel writing, autobiographies and online blogs. Remember to annotate as you read.

2 You should be able to **identify** and **explain** how the writer uses: language techniques, words and phrases and structural features, including sentence lengths.

3 You should show an ability to analyse when you **explain** and **evaluate** how the writer has crafted the text in a way that leaves an impression upon a reader. Phrases like these will help you:
   ● The reader infers...
   ● The writer successfully makes the reader...
   ● The reader appreciates that...
   ● These words force the reader to...
   ● The reader's response here is to...

4 Review your practice responses, and the feedback received from your teacher, to identify your strengths and targets for improvement.

annotate: to highlight, circle or underline important information within a text and write brief notes alongside the text to help record your ideas and observations

Task 3: Extracting meaning

What this question involves

Task 3 in Unit 1, Section B requires you to show your understanding of a text by locating the central meaning and **summarising** it using your own words.

> **summarise**: give an overview of the key points expressed within a text

Timing

You will have 12 minutes to complete this task and there are 12 marks available.

What is the examiner looking for?

The examiner wants to see that you can:
- understand the main points in a given text
- communicate the main ideas using your own words
- support your interpretation of the main ideas by selecting two pieces of relevant evidence for each point you make.

Summarising the main ideas

REVISED

Task 3 will require you to extract **two** key ideas or reasons from a text and summarise them using your own words. When attempting this task you should:
- highlight the key words in the question which will identify what information you are looking for
- read through the text, highlighting the relevant sections which contain the key ideas
- consider what is being stated and think about how you can express the same idea **concisely** and using your own words
- identify two quotations to support each idea/reason.

> **Exam tip**
>
> Avoid copying lengthy quotations from the passage – keep evidence short and relevant.

> **concise**: brief and succinct

Task

During an unsuccessful expedition to the South Pole in 1914, Ernest Shackleton's ship *The Endurance* was destroyed by pack ice. He and his crew then had to make the dangerous journey home on a small ship called *The Caird*.

Read this extract from Shackleton's account of his voyage and identify two reasons why the crew are feeling troubled.

> That day and the following day passed for us in a sort of nightmare. Our mouths were dry and our tongues were swollen. The wind was still strong and the heavy sea forced us to navigate carefully, but any thought of our peril from the waves was buried beneath the consciousness of our raging thirst. The bright moments were those when we each received our one mug of hot milk during the long, bitter watches of the night. Things were bad for us in those days, but the end was coming. The morning of May 8 broke thick and stormy, with squalls from the north-west. We searched the waters ahead for a sign of land, and though we could see nothing more than had met our eyes for many days, we were cheered by a sense that the goal was near at hand.
>
> From *South* by Ernest Shackleton

Mark scheme

There are 12 marks available for this question. There are 4 marks available for each reason and your ability to communicate using your own words. There are 2 marks available for providing two pieces of supporting evidence for each reason. In answering the above task, you should have commented on:

Why the crew are feeling troubled	Supporting evidence
They have had a few very difficult days which have affected their mood.	'That day and the following day passed for us in a sort of nightmare.'
The unfavourable weather conditions make sailing very difficult.	'The wind was still strong and the heavy sea forced us to navigate carefully...'
They are suffering from extreme thirst which is dominating their thoughts.	'...any thought of our peril from the waves was buried beneath the consciousness of our raging thirst.'
They are sleep-deprived and forced to keep alert during the night.	'...during the long, bitter watches of the night.'
They feel completely cut off from land and do not seem certain of their location.	'We searched the waters ahead for a sign of land, and though we could see nothing more than had met our eyes for many days...'

Below is an extract taken from a GCSE student's response. Read it and the comments which indicate what the student has done well.

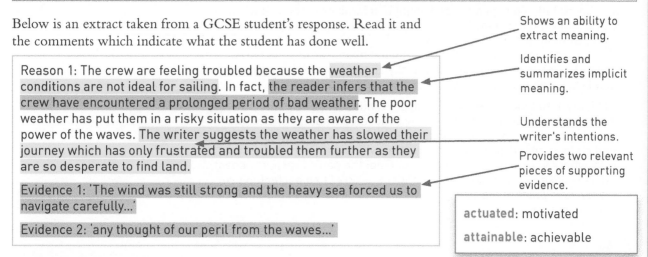

Reason 1: The crew are feeling troubled because the weather conditions are not ideal for sailing. In fact, the reader infers that the crew have encountered a prolonged period of bad weather. The poor weather has put them in a risky situation as they are aware of the power of the waves. The writer suggests the weather has slowed their journey which has only frustrated and troubled them further as they are so desperate to find land.

Evidence 1: 'The wind was still strong and the heavy sea forced us to navigate carefully...'

Evidence 2: 'any thought of our peril from the waves...'

Shows an ability to extract meaning.

Identifies and summarizes implicit meaning.

Understands the writer's intentions.

Provides two relevant pieces of supporting evidence.

actuated: motivated

attainable: achievable

Test yourself

TESTED ☐

Read the extract below which is taken from a statement delivered by Siegfried Sassoon in July 1917. Sassoon served in the First World War as a captain in the army and had been praised and decorated for his bravery and commitment to the cause.

In your own words write down **two** reasons the writer gives to explain his lack of support for the war. Present **two pieces** of supporting evidence for **each reason**.

I am making this statement as an act of wilful defiance of military authority because I believe that the war is being deliberately prolonged by those who have the power to end it.

I am a soldier, convinced that I am acting on behalf of soldiers. I believe that this war, upon which I entered as a war of defence and liberation, has now become a war of aggression and conquest. I believe that the purposes for which I and my fellow soldiers entered upon this war should have been so clearly stated as to have made it impossible to change them and that, had this been done, the objects which actuated us would now be attainable by negotiation.

I have seen and endured the sufferings of the troops and I can no longer be a party to prolong these sufferings for ends which I believe to be evil and unjust. I am not protesting against the conduct of the war, but against the political errors and insincerities for which the fighting men are being sacrificed.

Answers on pp. 91–92

How to prepare for the exam

You should create opportunities to develop your summarising skills.
- When listening to class presentations as part of Unit 2, practise summarising the main ideas communicated. Challenge yourself by trying to write a concise summary in less than one minute.
- At the end of lessons, summarise the main learning points on a Post-it note.
- Have a go summarising the plot of your favourite films or books in less than 50 words.
- Locate suitable extracts and devise a suitable Task 3 question to accompany your chosen extract. Practise responding under timed conditions and assess your efforts against the mark scheme above.

Supporting interpretations

REVISED

When you extract meaning from a text you must prove the accuracy of your interpretation by providing evidence from the text.

Read the extract below where the writer is describing the experience of getting lost whilst out on a hill walk with his wife.

> To this day, I still don't know why I didn't speak up earlier. For at least an hour I'd carried a gnawing doubt that we had somehow gone off route, but dutifully I'd kept my wife distracted from our predicament with small talk. I'd hoped to catch sight of a familiar landmark which would allow me to get my bearings and set us back on the planned route, without her ever having to worry. It didn't happen. Instead we both became unusually quiet and continued hiking across the hills, pretending not to feel anxious as the sky above darkened and the clouds seemed to move in on us.
>
> Suddenly, it felt like we were adrift from civilisation. The path had completely disappeared, the thick fog concealed what lay ahead and the rain drizzled down, dampening any optimism we'd managed to hold on to up to this point. It didn't matter which direction we looked; everywhere we turned was grey. I could feel the panic rise in my chest but as I spoke my voice sounded confident; a skill I had perfected over twenty-four years of marriage. It was my responsibility to get us back safely to our car.

Task

Find evidence from the text to support each of the points below:
(a) The husband feels responsible for the fact he and his wife got lost.
(b) The wife knows they are lost.
(c) The husband can remain calm in a crisis.
(d) The couple have a strong marriage.

Typical mistake

Students often fail to put their textual evidence inside quotation marks.

1 Read the extract below where the writer recounts the experience of starting school.

I wasn't ready for this act of abandonment. For the first four years of my life, I had relied upon my mother offering her hand to reassure me, to let me know she was always there and would never leave me. On that traumatic September afternoon, everything changed. Mum was prising her hand out of my vice-like grip. She was smiling but her voice was full of anxiety and her eyes were full of tears.

I remember busily colouring in a picture for Mum to add to her 'gallery' which she proudly displayed on the kitchen walls. Looking up, I caught sight of Mum and the stranger chatting. The stranger was pointing to the door and held Mum by the elbow. The next thing I remember is seeing the back of Mum as she walked out of the classroom. 'Mum,' I yelled, holding up my latest masterpiece, so certain it would stop her in her tracks, send her running in my direction to scoop me up and take us both to the park. She didn't look back. She kept on walking.

I struggled to make sense of what was happening. Mum was leaving me with a complete stranger; it felt like the ultimate betrayal. 'Mum will be back soon,' said the stranger, smiling, but it wasn't a 'Mum' smile; it was the same smile she had for all the other crying kids. 'Soon.' What did that mean? What four year old understands the word 'soon'?

The stranger approached me, 'Mum will be back soon,' she repeated, but already she had an eye on the boy throwing sand at the opposite side of the room.

Find evidence from the passage which supports the following points:

Summary	Evidence
The child and his mother have a strong relationship.	
This event has been a defining moment in the life of the writer.	
The child feels let down by his mother.	
The experience is an emotional one for the child.	
The experience is an emotional one for the mother.	
The teacher is not a very empathetic individual.	

2 Task 3 in Unit 1, Section B, tests your ability to extract meaning by summarising *and* supporting your interpretation with relevant supporting evidence.

Read again the extract above and answer the question:
In your own words write down two reasons the writer gives to explain why this was such a memorable occasion. Present two pieces of evidence for each reason.

Answers on pp. 92–93

Task 4: Reading media texts

What this question involves

Media texts are non-fiction texts but they communicate meaning through language, structural and presentational features. Task 4 requires you to analyse how **language** is used in a media text.

Timing

You will have 17 minutes to complete this task and there are 20 marks available.

What is the examiner looking for?

The examiner wants to see that you can:

- recognise how the writer achieves their purpose through language – specific language devices and words and phrases used
- correctly identify a range of language devices used by the writer
- select relevant quotations from the text
- explain the effect of language choices upon a reader
- provide a full consideration of the text by covering the beginning, middle and end.

Persuasive language

REVISED

Many media texts are produced to promote products, experiences or places. Organisations and businesses produce media texts to attract an audience in the hope that they will gain their custom and their money, so they rely heavily on persuasive language.

> **Exam tip**
>
> You should be able to identify these techniques:
> - **P** Promotions
> - **E** Expert opinion/reviews
> - **R** Rhetorical devices
> - **S** Superlatives
> - **U** Use of factual information
> - **A** Adjectives
> - **D** Direct address
> - **E** Exaggeration

Rhetoric

REVISED

Rhetoric is the art of using language to persuade. It involves using language which will leave an impact on the heart and mind of the audience. Rhetorical devices include: rhetorical questions; alliteration; repetition; lists of three and exaggeration.

Task

Read the extract below and highlight examples of rhetorical language. Try to explain how each rhetorical device is used to leave an impression upon a reader:

> What makes Animal Haven different from other animal sanctuaries? Here at Animal Haven we believe our furry friends bring more laughter, more love and more energy into our lives. We know that your pet is part of your family, and as a VIP (Very Important Pet) at Animal Haven, they become part of our family. Before your pet makes a reservation, we work closely with you to ensure they will enjoy the same food, the same exercise routine and the same treats. We understand pets and owners can suffer from separation anxiety and we seek to minimise this through familiarisation meetings and assigning a member of our dedicated team to personally look after your precious pet. With spacious sleeping areas, extensive exercise lawns and animal-loving staff, your pet will be in heaven at Animal Haven!

Fact and opinion

REVISED

Media texts can make bold statements to influence the reader's response. Factual statements can be used to make the reader feel informed about the organisation or the product. For example, a text to promote a restaurant might refer to awards the establishment has won. A hotel might inform the reader of the number of rooms or the distance from the nearest town; for example, 'Londonderry is only 12 miles away and offers plenty of shopping opportunities.' Notice the inclusion of the word 'only' to make the reader feel the hotel is in a prime location.

Opinions can also be included; for example, a book cover will often include positive statements from reviews which will act as an endorsement and encourage a potential reader to pick up the book. Sometimes opinions will be disguised as fact; for example, 'The best diner in town' or 'A must-read for fans of fantasy fiction!'

> **Exam tip**
>
> Media texts usually employ an assertive and positive tone as they want the reader to have confidence in their organisation and/or their product.

> **Exam tip**
>
> Notice how exclamation marks can be used to add emphasis and convey strong emotions such as excitement.

Task

Read the extract below. Write a short paragraph to explain how the writer makes use of fact and opinion.

> With our one wedding policy, Manor Rose House is the perfect wedding venue for the bride and groom who want to give their guests a day to remember. With packages starting from only £3000 – including complimentary table arrangements and a champagne reception on arrival – there is no better place to celebrate your special day. Our spectacular gardens provide a breath-taking backdrop for your wedding photographs. Let Manor Rose House give you the wedding of your dreams.
>
> 'We are so pleased we chose to celebrate our wedding at Manor Rose House, the location is stunning and the staff were amazing.' – Mr and Mrs Jones

Promotional language

REVISED

Promotional language has strong appeal because it entices the audience by making them feel they can take part in something special or benefit from a limited offer. Promotional language will often do the following:
- **Describe** what the audience can expect from the organisation; for example, 'Enjoy stepping back in time with a visit to the National Museum.'

- **Imperative verbs** are used to compel the reader to take action based upon what they have read; for example, 'Book your tickets today to get 20 per cent off.'
- Use **adjectives** to influence the reader's impression. Adjectives can be positive or negative so they will be carefully chosen depending on the effect the writer wants to achieve; for example, 'Relax in our luxurious spa. At night, dine in our fine restaurant where our award-winning chef will prepare your meal using only fresh, locally produced ingredients.'
- **Exaggerate** the experience the reader can expect; for example, 'We will guarantee a day you will never forget. A truly magical experience awaits all visitors.'
- Encourage the reader to form positive impressions by including **reviews** from previously satisfied customers; for example, 'The perfect day out for the family, the kids didn't want to leave.'
- Include **statistical** information to make the reader feel informed or to draw their attention to discounted offers; for example, 'Limited offer, save 25 per cent by booking online.'
- Include **superlatives** to influence the expectations of the reader; for example, 'The greatest day out for first-class family fun.'
- Encourage the reader to think or feel a particular way by using **emotive language**; for example, 'Relax and spoil yourself by indulging in one of our treatments delivered by our team of body experts. Following a consultation, we will prescribe a bespoke treatment to guarantee younger, smoother, firmer skin. We will literally turn back time. All our treatments are natural and kind to sensitive skin.'

Tasks

1 Look again at the blue emboldened phrases in the examples above. Explain what impact each of the highlighted word/phrases will have upon a reader.

2 Read the extract below taken from a media text to promote an outdoor activity centre.

> The staff at Adventure Outdoor Activity Centre would like you to visit. We will try to make your experience fun and exciting. We think we are a good place for families to spend a day having fun in a safe environment. All equipment will be provided and if you book online we will reduce your bill by 25 per cent. We are very pleased to report that 90 per cent of customers would recommend us to their friends and family.

This writer has not been very successful in using promotional language. Rewrite the paragraph to make it more persuasive.

Language to connect and engage a reader

REVISED

Direct address means to 'talk' to your reader and make them feel involved. By addressing the reader directly, writers make the reader feel that the text holds relevance for them. Direct address can create a conversational tone which will help to engage the reader.

Writers can engage a reader using various methods:

- Using personal and inclusive pronouns. The personal pronoun 'you' is commonly used in media texts to connect with and engage the reader. Inclusive pronouns such as 'we', 'us' and 'our' make the reader feel part of a group and can emphasise the commitment of the organisation to satisfy the needs of their customer; for example, 'Our staff work hard to deliver high-quality service. We are proud of our customer service awards.'
- Using questions to engage the reader by making them think; for example, 'Are you looking for a fun day out for the entire family?'

Task

Read the extract below which has been taken from a brochure to promote a children's play park. Comment on how the techniques and phrases in bold help persuade the reader that this would be a good place to host a children's party:

Wonder-World invite **you** to celebrate your special day with us. You and your guests can enjoy **two fun-filled** hours **in Ireland's number one** indoor playground. Our **newest** attraction, 'The Accelerator', is the **ultimate** endurance test and **will guarantee endless fun**. **Will you cross the finish line and secure a place on our 'Wall of Achievement'? Let us** take the stress out of organising your party with **first-class catering**; our menu caters for all dietary needs and delivers **delicious and nutritious** food. **Ninety-five per cent** of customers have rated our birthday packages as five star! **Book today** and **discover** what makes Wonder-World wonderful!

Wonder-World is the place where dreams come true. Call us today to secure your booking. Groups of 15 or more benefit from a 10 per cent discount.

Consider this extract from a GCSE student's response:

> The writer begins by addressing the reader directly by using the personal pronoun in the phrase, 'Wonder-World invite you to celebrate your special day with us.' The reader is made to feel this text is relevant to them through the use of the personal pronoun 'you'. They give the impression they want to be part of their customers' celebrations by using inclusive language '...celebrate your special day with us'. By opening the extract with a conversational tone, the writer makes the reader feel engaged and the phrase 'special day' makes the reader feel that this is a place where they are valued and important. The reader is made to feel more than a customer as the text refers to them and fellow customers as 'guests'. This successfully makes the reader think the organisation offers a high standard of customer service.

Exam tip

Consider where certain techniques are used within a text. Pay close attention to how the writer chooses to begin their text to hook the reader. Also look at how they choose to end by leaving a lasting impression upon a reader.

Exam tip

When explaining try to avoid ending on a quotation. Quotations should be 'wrapped' in your commentary. Remember P.E.E.

Assessment comment

This candidate offers a confident analysis of the writer's methods and intentions. They correctly identify language techniques and their impact upon a reader. They zoom in on specific use of language and they select relevant quotations to support their analysis.

Mark scheme

Use the mark scheme below to assess your response to the above task:

Level 1	A simple attempt to offer some basic comments on the writer's craft.
	May offer some selection of relevant evidence.
Level 2	A straightforward recognition of the writer's craft which considers some language choices and/or language techniques.
	Straightforward understanding with some attempt to select relevant evidence to support interpretations.
Level 3	A generally focused consideration of the writer's craft with some analysis of language.
	Recognises how some of the writer's intentions have been communicated through language choices.
	Generally accurate selection of evidence linked to appropriate explanations.
Level 4	A more analytical response which explores and evaluates some language strategies.
	A range of mostly accurate evidence is used to explore in some detail, the methods and intentions of the writer.
Level 5	An assured analysis which confidently identifies a range of appropriate features.
	An assured selection of precise evidence which is used to support confident analysis of the writer's methods and intentions.

Test yourself

Below is an extract taken from a hotel brochure. Comment on how language has been used to convey the impression that this would be a good place for a relaxing break.

> Are you looking for the perfect short stay to recharge your batteries? Only 18 miles outside of Dublin, the Grand Garden Hotel is the perfect base for a tranquil weekend break. Nestled in 18 acres of stunning woodland, the Grand Garden is a luxurious hideaway. This former linen mill has been totally transformed with spacious rooms, an award-winning spa and breath-taking views. We make it our mission that you can unwind and de-stress. You cannot fail to fall in love with the Grand Garden. Enjoy mingling with friends in our exotic roof-terraced restaurant and try our 'Taster Menu' with a delicious starter, main and dessert for only €20 per person. Breakfast is served until 12.30 so you can enjoy a well-deserved lie-in and check out is not until 2.00pm so you can soak up all the hotel has to offer. Create memories you will cherish for a lifetime, make every minute count and enjoy the spectacular food and facilities on offer at the Grand Garden Hotel – your body and mind will thank you for it.

Answers on p. 93

How to prepare for the exam

Read as many media texts as you can. Practise spotting rhetorical devices, persuasive language and language to connect. Try writing an analysis in 15–17 minutes.

Practise writing and reading a range of persuasive texts. If you take on the responsibility of a writer, you will begin to appreciate the craft of other writers. Get used to reading closely so you stop to appreciate the writer's intentions.

Review your practice tasks, including the feedback offered by your teacher. Identify what you do well and how you can improve your analysis of media texts.

Task 5: Analysing presentational features

What this task involves

Task 5 requires you to study a section of a media text, select two presentational features and explain their impact upon a reader.

Timing

You will have 8 minutes to complete this task and there are 10 marks available – including 1 mark for identifying each presentational feature and 4 marks for explaining its impact upon a reader.

What is the examiner looking for?

The examiner wants to see that you can:
- appreciate how the purpose of a text is achieved through presentational features
- explain how colour, layout, image and/or font convey meaning to a reader
- select two presentational devices and precisely explain their impact upon a reader.

Presentational features

As well as communicating through language, media texts use presentational features to communicate with their target audience. Just as language is carefully chosen, the creators of media texts also make careful decisions about:
- the colour(s) used within the text
- layout features
- images
- fonts.

> **Exam tip**
>
> Use C.L.I.F. (Colour, Layout, Image and Font) to help you remember what you should consider when analysing presentational features.

These presentational devices are used to:
- gain the reader's attention – remember we often encounter media texts as we go about our everyday business so they should be eye-catching
- establish a mood or expectation – colours, images and font will often inform our first impressions of a media text
- help the reader remember information – layout features help the reader navigate the text and retain key information.

Analysing colour

Colour is often the presentational feature which first draws our attention to a media text. The creators of media texts know that different colours carry certain **connotations**.

> **connotation**: an idea or feeling associated with a colour; for example, yellow has connotations of warmth and summer so is regarded as a positive colour

Task

Make a list of connotations which you associate with each of the following colours:

Colour	Connotations
Black	
White	
Red	
Green	
Blue	
Orange	
Purple	

It is common for media texts to employ a specific colour scheme, limited to a few dominant colours, but sometimes they will employ a wide variety of colours to achieve a rainbow or kaleidoscopic effect. You should not try to analyse each individual colour, instead acknowledge that a variety of colours have been used and explain the intended effect. Often a wide range of colours suggest the organisation is vibrant or the experience will offer the audience a variety of things to see and do, making it exciting.

Task

Study the text below and opposite. Write a paragraph analysing how colour has been used in this leaflet.

If you are an employer or manager responsible for people whose work keeps them outside for most of the day, please read this leaflet. It gives advice on reducing the health risks for your employees when they are working in the sun.

Exposure to ultraviolet (UV) radiation from the sun can cause skin damage including sunburn, blistering, skin ageing and in the long term can lead to skin cancer. Skin cancer is the most common form of cancer in the UK, with over 40 000 new cases diagnosed each year.

UV radiation should be considered an occupational hazard for people who work outdoors.

Who is at risk?

- People with pale skin are most at risk of skin damage, especially those with fair or red hair, with a lot of freckles or with a family history of skin cancer.
- People with brown or black skin are at low risk but people of all skin colours can suffer from overheating and dehydration.

As an employer you can...

- Include sun protection advice in routine health and safety training. Inform workers that a tan is not healthy – it is a sign that skin has already been damaged by the sun.
- Encourage workers to keep covered up during the summer months – especially at lunch time when the sun is at its hottest. They can cover up with a long-sleeved shirt, and a hat with a brim or flap that protects the ears and neck.
- Encourage workers to use sunscreen of at least SPF (Sun Protection Factor) 15 on any part of the body they can't cover up and to apply it as directed on the product. They might prefer to use a spray or an alcohol-based (non-greasy) sunscreen.

- Encourage workers to take their breaks in the shade, if possible, rather than staying out in the sun.
- Consider scheduling work to minimise exposure.
- Site water points and rest areas in the shade.
- Encourage workers to drink plenty of water to avoid dehydration.
- Keep your workers informed about the dangers of sun exposure – make use of the Health and Safety Executive (HSE) leaflet *Keep your top on* (see 'Further information').
- Encourage workers to check their skin regularly for unusual spots or moles that change size, shape or colour and to seek medical advice promptly if they find anything that causes them concern.

Consulting your employees and their safety representatives is important. Take their views into account when introducing any new sun safety initiatives.

What are the benefits to your company?

- Fewer absence days through sunburn.
- A healthier and better-informed workforce.
- Reduced risk to employees of skin cancer from long-term sun exposure.

From www.hse.gov.uk/pubns/indg337.pdf

Analysing layout

REVISED

As we tend to encounter media texts unexpectedly, it is important that we can extract and retain important information. Imagine how difficult it would be to process the information in a take away menu if there were no lists, no bullet points, no images and all the information was presented as one block of text! A reader will not be attracted to a text which intimidates them or appears to be overloaded with information. The appearance of a text can indicate the intended audience; if it appears to include a lot of information then it is likely to be targeted at an adult audience, whereas a lot of cartoon images might suggest a younger audience is being targeted.

> **Exam tip**
>
> Layout features should be obvious without having to 'read' the text in any great detail.

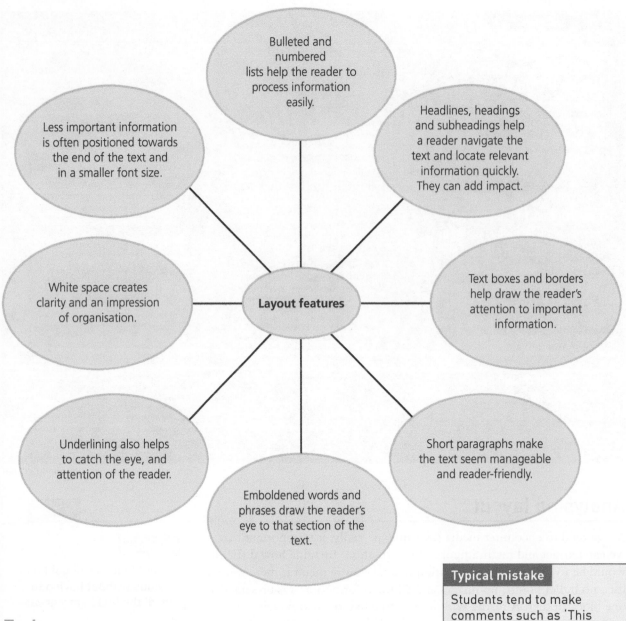

Layout features

- Bulleted and numbered lists help the reader to process information easily.
- Headlines, headings and subheadings help a reader navigate the text and locate relevant information quickly. They can add impact.
- Less important information is often positioned towards the end of the text and in a smaller font size.
- Text boxes and borders help draw the reader's attention to important information.
- White space creates clarity and an impression of organisation.
- Short paragraphs make the text seem manageable and reader-friendly.
- Underlining also helps to catch the eye, and attention of the reader.
- Emboldened words and phrases draw the reader's eye to that section of the text.

Task

Study the leaflet on sun safety on pages 46 and 47. Write a paragraph analysing how layout features have been used in this text.

> **Typical mistake**
>
> Students tend to make comments such as 'This makes it eye-catching' but then fail to explain how. Be precise with your analysis.

Analysing images

REVISED

Images have an important role in any media text, as they are often the first thing that grabs our attention. Think of how many times you have judged a book by its cover! Images do much more than simply grab our attention and media texts rely on them as an important means of communication.

To analyse precisely you should consider what the images in the text in front of you are communicating about the organisation, the product or the place.

Tasks

1 Decide which of the images opposite would be the best to include in a leaflet about healthy eating:

2 Language and images tend to work together to have maximum impact upon a reader. A media text advertising a holiday resort includes the claim:

Explore stunning beaches which stretch for miles.

Decide which of the images on page 50 would best accompany the sentence above:

As well as studying the content of an image you should also think about the camera perspective or angle and the framing of the shot.

Task

Study the images below which have been taken from a media text to advertise a nature reserve:

Exam tip

If the text includes more than one image you should acknowledge this but select one which you feel is most effective in communicating to the reader.

Bird's eye view to make the attraction seem vast and make the reader think there will be lots to explore. Will appeal to those who enjoy the outdoors.

Close-up shot to allow the reader to appreciate that this is a special place to get up close to nature.

Medium shot to include several people and make the reader think this is a place for the family to spend time together.

The image below was taken from a media text promoting an animal sanctuary. Write a paragraph explaining how the image presents the sanctuary as a caring place.

Analysing font

REVISED

Most *students* are NOT *reading* enough!

If **you** want *to* **succeed**, you **must** *read.*

As you can see from the above, there are a variety of **font** styles and sizes which can be used within texts. Most media texts will favour a font which can be easily read.

font: the size and shape of the writing or copy within a text

Task

Decide which of the font styles above could be described as:

● easily read
● modern
● traditional
● sophisticated
● playful.

> **Exam tip**
>
> Titles and product names often have a different font size and style from the rest of the text. A larger font size helps the information stand out but the font style can often be linked to the subject of the media text.

Font size

Different font sizes help to make a text visually appealing. Remember most readers do not read a media text from beginning to end, instead they scan it and extract key ideas. A variety of font sizes and styles will appeal to readers who scan the text quickly.

Font style

> **Exam tip**
>
> When describing font style, try to think of a suitable adjective to describe it. Ask yourself: is it original? Striking? Modern? Traditional?

Task

Study the statements below, which have all been taken from media texts. Study them carefully and decide what the font style suggests about the product, place or organisation being promoted.

Jungle-mania (A children's indoor play barn)

The Blood Sucker (An attraction at a theme park)

CASTLE MUSEUM (A museum)

Chocolicious (A chocolate drink)

Test yourself

Study the text below. Select two presentational devices and explain how they make the reader think this will be an enjoyable experience.

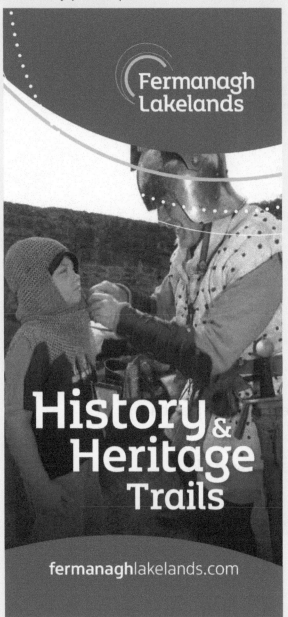

From www.fermanaghlakelands.com/Portals/0/downloads/FLTHistoryTrail.pdf

Answers on pp. 93–94

How to prepare for the exam

You are surrounded by media texts which offer you a chance to develop your skills in reading and analysing these texts. Study cinema posters, computer game covers, book covers, advertisements in magazines and even any junk mail which comes through your door; identify what decisions have been made regarding presentational devices.

Remember you will be asked to select two presentational devices so practise reading a variety of texts and selecting two features you can best analyse.

Producing your own media text will help you appreciate the decisions which must be made to ensure the text achieves its purpose and catches the attention of an audience.

What does Unit 4, Section A involve?

What is being assessed?

Section A is assessing your writing skills. This means you are being assessed on the quality and accuracy of your written work.

What will you have to write?

You will have a choice of task in this section. There will be two tasks offered: one Personal Writing task and one Creative Writing task. You will choose and complete **one** task.

If you choose the Creative Writing task, there will be an image provided on which you must base your story.

How long do you have?

You have 55 minutes in which to complete one task. It is advised that you spend up to 15 minutes planning for writing, 30 minutes writing your response and 10 minutes checking over and editing your work.

How many marks are available?

The total number of marks available in Section A is 88. Up to 58 marks are available for producing an organised and interesting piece of writing which matches form with purpose to engage the interest of a reader. Up to 30 marks are available for using a range of sentence structures and accurate spelling, punctuation and grammar.

How much are you expected to write?

As in Unit 1, Section A you are expected to produce an extended response but you should prioritise producing a well-crafted **narrative** which engages your reader. Aim to write something you would enjoy reading!

> **narrative:** a story or account of real or imaginary events and experiences

Purpose, audience and form

REVISED

Before beginning to write you should be clear about the following:
- Why you are writing – your purpose.
- Who you are writing for – your audience.
- The form your writing will take.

The examiner is looking for a response that:
- clearly meets the demands of the set task
- is well organised and engaging
- shows an awareness of audience, purpose and form
- uses a range of linguistic devices, well-chosen vocabulary and a variety of sentence structures to add interest.

> **Exam tip**
>
> Remember your writing may have more than one purpose; for example, you will want to **inform** your reader about events and **describe** in detail what took place and how you/your characters reacted.

Task

Below are two sample writing tasks – one Personal Writing and one Creative Writing task. Identify the purpose, audience and form for each task.

○ Write a personal essay for the examiner about a time you had to show responsibility.

OR

○ Write a creative essay which would be included in a collection of stories for teenage readers. Your response should be based on the picture below. Provide a title for your story.

Planning for writing

An examiner will recognise a good piece of writing which has been well planned. Planning is an important part of the writing process so ensure you spend time deciding:

- what you will write about
- what details your reader needs to know
- how you will engage your reader
- how you will organise your ideas.

You should have had practice in planning and know which planning method works best for you. Popular planning methods include: the spider diagram; the bullet-point list; the flowchart and the story-tree.

> **Exam tip**
>
> Planning should look untidy. Your plan is not for the examiner, it is for you, so there is no need for full sentences or to actually write out parts of your response.

> **Typical mistake**
>
> Many students fail to plan effectively. They begin writing without carefully considering **what** they want to write and **how** they want to tell their story. This often results in them running out of time and/or ideas.

> **Typical mistake**
>
> Students often plan about what they want to write, but they fail to think carefully enough about **how** they will communicate their ideas to the reader. Think carefully about the different techniques you will use and when they will be best employed throughout your writing.

Task

Select one of the sample tasks on the previous page and produce a plan which will help you write an extended response which is detailed, descriptive and engages the reader.

Structuring your writing

REVISED ☐

Organising your ideas is also part of the planning process. In a successful narrative, the ideas expressed should be connected and shared with the reader in a way that aids their understanding and increases their interest.

The examiner is looking for:
- writing that is organised into paragraphs
- paragraphs that are connected so the narrative is developed in a coherent and interesting way.

Depending on the form of your Personal or Creative Writing, you are likely to use a **chronological** or a **flashback structure**.

> **Exam tip**
>
> In chronological writing the tense is usually consistent – when recounting an experience, the past tense is used. A creative response may favour the present tense to inject a sense of immediacy.

In the extract below the student writes chronologically about a memorable holiday:

> **chronological structure:** organising your writing by relating events in the order in which they happened; when writing chronologically, it is important to be selective about what information your reader needs to know and then tell those details in a way that is descriptive and interesting
>
> **flashback structure:** taking your reader back in time so they can understand the significance of present feelings or experiences; the events told in the past will connect to the present

> We arrived at our hotel which was lovely. We got out of the taxi and the taxi man got our suitcases out of the boot of his car. There were four heavy suitcases but the taxi man would not let my dad help him. My dad paid the taxi man as the rest of us climbed the steps and went to find the hotel reception.
>
> Inside, the hotel was like a palace, it was golden and glittering; I felt like a celebrity. A smiling receptionist welcomed us and got all our details off mum. She showed our passports and our booking reservation. The receptionist gave us some leaflets about the hotel and nearby attractions. I carried the leaflets. Dad then arrived. He nudged me, 'What ya think son? Gorgeous isn't it.' I could tell he was so proud to be treating us all to a place like this. I replied, 'It sure is dad, a world away from the old caravan in Portrush.' We both laughed.

Mark scheme

Level 1	Limited development of ideas with simple descriptions and few language techniques.
	Simple awareness of purpose, audience and form.
Level 2	Some successful communication and development of ideas with attempts to use language techniques which are fitting for audience and purpose.
	Sensible organisation of ideas which, in places, might be linked by structural features.
Level 3	Mostly successful communication and development of original ideas and descriptions.
	Uses language techniques with increasing success to gain the interest of the audience.
	Successful organisation of ideas with clear evidence of structural features.

Level 4	Communicates and develops ideas in a way that is original and convincing.
	Successfully uses a variety of language techniques throughout the response to enhance the engagement of the reader.
	Skilful organisation of ideas.
Level 5	Highly confident development of ideas in a style which is highly engaging and successfully hooks and holds the reader's interest.
	Confidently employs a full range of language techniques which are used precisely to make the writing original and compelling.
	Assured organisation of ideas with structural features.

Assessment comment

The student response on page 57 successfully communicates ideas and, in places, attempts to describe by using adjectives and a simile. They successfully integrate direct speech in an attempt to add interest. Overall, they fail to successfully select ideas that will add interest to the story and so it lacks originality. This is a Level 2 response.

Tasks

1 Look again at the student response on page 57. Identify what should be omitted and where the student has missed opportunities to add description.
2 Rewrite the passage so it is more interesting and succeeds in holding the attention of the reader.
3 In the extract below the writer makes use of flashback structure:

> Standing on the shoreline, she closed her eyes and breathed deeply. Suddenly it all came back to her; that fateful day ten years ago when she had discovered the truth about who she was. She could vividly recall the stunned reaction of her 'family' when they realised she had abandoned the rock pools, quietly made her way back and had heard every word spoken. She would never forget the horror on their faces and the heavy silence. She did the only thing she could, she ran towards the sea. Now here she was, once again running towards the sea, with arms outstretched, but today she carried no trauma, no feelings of deceit or abandonment. Today she felt victorious.

Now read this opening to a story. Continue the paragraph by inserting a flashback and then reverting back to present tense:

> It had been years since I had last been inside my old school. I had been surprised when the letter had arrived inviting me back, but I jumped at the opportunity to return and share my story with the pupils. Of course, back when I was a boy, no one ever told me I'd be inspirational...

Typical mistake

Candidates **inform** the reader about their chosen experience, communicating what happened and why but, without description, it fails to interest and engage the reader.

Exam tip

When using a flashback structure, you should be confident in managing tenses. You might begin in the present tense, shift to the past and conclude back in the present.

Personal Writing

The Personal Writing task will require you to write about something you have direct experience of. Remember though that you are writing for an audience and a reader will want to read something that is interesting and engaging. This is not an easy task, so it is important that you use the recommended 15 minutes to plan in detail what you want to write about, how ideas are connected and how you will ensure your reader is engaged in your narrative.

> **Exam tip**
>
> Writing from your own experience will make your writing **authentic** and convincing but remember you are only writing a short story so be selective about what you share.

authentic: realistic and believable

Narrative perspective

REVISED

As personal writing requires you to write about yourself, you will use a first-person perspective. The benefit of a first-person narration is that the reader is given access to the narrator's inner thoughts and feelings, so the reader can **empathise**.

empathise: understand and share the feelings of another

Tasks

The extract below is written using a first-person perspective. The writer recounts getting into trouble at school:

> 'Boyd, get your pathetic self to the office at once.' Master Warren sneered down at me, unable to hide his delight that I was in trouble ... big trouble.
>
> I jumped at the sound of my name. I had been waiting for this summons to the principal's office but suddenly I began to feel sick. My stomach churned like a blender on high-speed. It felt like every eye in the room was on me. Making my way out of the classroom, I could hear their whispers. Some boys lifted textbooks to cover their mouths, but their eyes followed me right to the door. Of course, I could hear them and I knew what they were saying, 'There he goes again' and 'Will he ever learn?'
>
> Making my way to the principal's office I too asked myself that same question, 'Will I ever learn?' I had gained a reputation as being a bit of a trouble magnet but this time even I knew I had gone too far.

1 What sort of a character is the narrator?
2 Identify the different feelings the narrator experiences in the extract.
3 How would this account differ if it was told from an **omniscient perspective**?
4 How has the writer made this an interesting narrative?

omniscient perspective: the narrator is detached from the events and tells the story from an all-knowing perspective

Openings

REVISED

Openings are important as they need to engage the reader and establish a strong first impression. There are a variety of ways to begin your Personal Writing such as: using dialogue; asking a question; using an anecdote; using a descriptive opening or beginning with some dramatic action.

Task

Read the sample openings and, using the suggestions above, identify which approach is being used to begin these Personal Writing essays:

Opening	What introductory approach is used by the writer?
The grey sea was rough and angry. It spat out salty foam and seemed to roar at us as though warning us to stay out but its power was intoxicating.	
Those who know me well would probably describe me as a worrier. I stress over the smallest things, but nothing stresses me more than exams. As you can imagine I have spent the past few months in a permanent state of anxiety.	
'You can't be an astronaut,' cackled the careers advisor, throwing her head back and lightly hitting me on the arm as though I'd just cracked a joke. 'Why not?' I enquired. She stared. Realising it wasn't a joke she cleared her throat and started tapping her keyboard.	
It was past midnight when the knock on the door woke me from my sleep. It was an urgent, desperate knocking. The knock of someone in trouble ... or someone delivering troubling news.	
Have you ever been stopped in your tracks by something so mesmerising and magical?	

Adding interest

REVISED

Once you have decided what to write about, you should consider how you will tell your narrative in a way that interests your reader so that they want to continue reading.

Typical mistake

Students often feel their own experiences are not exciting enough to share with a reader or examiner but most professional writers are inspired by their own everyday experiences.

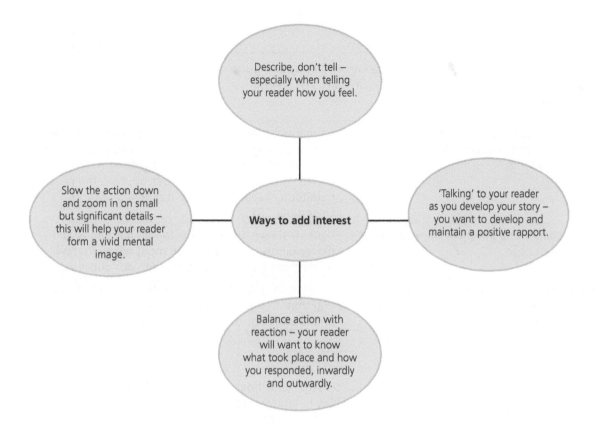

Describe, don't tell – especially when telling your reader how you feel.

Slow the action down and zoom in on small but significant details – this will help your reader form a vivid mental image.

Ways to add interest

'Talking' to your reader as you develop your story – you want to develop and maintain a positive rapport.

Balance action with reaction – your reader will want to know what took place and how you responded, inwardly and outwardly.

Task

Read the extract below taken from a student's response to the task: 'A memorable celebration'. Identify where the student has used the four approaches suggested above, to add interest:

> I brooded about for most of the morning, convinced my nearest and dearest had forgotten my birthday. I found all sorts of excuses to keep going downstairs and into the company of my parents, hoping that the sheer sight of me would cause them to remember and launch into a rendition of 'Happy Birthday.' Instead Mum carried on reading her newspaper and Dad was channel-surfing. I was invisible! My mind whirled with the reality of the situation – for them my birthday wasn't even worth remembering never mind celebrating!
>
> Up in my room, I slouched on the bed, cradled my pillow and tortured myself with depressing thoughts. Tears pooled in my eyes and trickled down my cheeks and onto my chin. I kept sniffing, as though I wanted to hold onto all of my sadness. Outside it was a scorching day and ordinarily I'd have been out in the garden kicking the football around or filling up the paddling pool. Not today. Today I moped about like I'd lost a winning lottery ticket and wallowed in self-pity. I must admit, I probably looked pretty pathetic and selfish, but please don't judge me – I was five!

Identify where this student uses:
- impressive vocabulary
- long or short sentences for effect
- punctuation to enhance meaning
- a simile
- alliteration.

Exam tip

This is Personal Writing but try to avoid starting every sentence with 'I + verb'. Use a variety of sentence starters.

Endings

You will want to end strongly so that you leave a lasting impression upon your reader. There are a number of ways to conclude personal writing, such as the following:

Reflect back on the situation or event to share your thoughts and feelings or consider how you have been influenced by what occurred.	As someone who is now older and wiser, I can look back and laugh at my own foolishness and will even admit that I over-reacted. Don't get me wrong, I don't regret a single thing, after all, I am the person I am today because of what happened back in December 2015.
Question your reader and get them thinking about what they have just read.	I guess life would be dull without challenges and disappointments. Surely you must agree that we learn more from our failures than our successes?
Inspire and motivate your reader by using imperative verbs and encouraging them to learn from your experiences.	There is only one thing we can take from this story and that is to get up every day, believe in yourself and follow your dream. If I can do it, so can you!

Exam tip

Try to avoid using 'In conclusion…' or 'To conclude…' to begin your final paragraph. It may be logical but it's not very original. Try to show more flair and be more creative about how your final paragraph will begin.

imperative verbs: orders or commanding verbs

Task

Using the above suggestions, write three different conclusions for the task: 'A time I challenged myself'.

Test yourself

TESTED

Using what you have learned about planning, adding interest, openings and endings, write a four-paragraph response to the task: Write a personal essay about a place you would like to live.

Answers on pp. 94–95

Creative Writing

Like Personal Writing, the Creative Writing task requires you to write a narrative that interests your reader and which demonstrates your skill as a writer to write accurately and make decisions about language choices and structural features.

As with Personal Writing, you will begin by identifying the purpose, audience and form of your writing. You will then spend up to 15 minutes planning and organising your ideas.

The examiner is looking for a response that:
- is interesting and original
- develops ideas and includes descriptive details
- is organised
- is accurate.

Creating a character

REVISED

As a writer, you will control the reader's impressions of the characters you create. When creating characters, you will consider their:
- physical appearance
- personality
- actions and behaviours
- voice: what they say and how
- relationships with others
- thoughts and attitudes, and others' thoughts about them.

Look at this description of the Artful Dodger from *Oliver Twist*, written by Charles Dickens:

> He was a **snub-nosed**, flat-browed, common-faced boy enough; and as dirty a juvenile as one would wish to see; but he had about him all the airs and manners of a man. He was short of his age: with rather bowlegs, and little, sharp, ugly eyes. His hat was stuck on the top of his head so lightly, that it threatened to fall off every moment – and would have done so, very often, if the wearer had not had a knack of every now and then giving his head a sudden twitch, which brought it back to its old place again. He wore a man's coat, which reached nearly to his heels. He had turned the cuffs back, half-way up his arm, to get his hands out of the sleeves: apparently with the ultimate view of thrusting them into the pockets of his corduroy trousers; for there he kept them. He was, altogether, as **roystering** and swaggering a young gentleman as ever stood four feet six, or something less, in his **bluchers**.
>
> 'Hullo, my covey! What's the row?' said this strange young gentleman to Oliver.
>
> 'I am very hungry and tired,' replied Oliver: the tears standing in his eyes as he spoke. 'I have walked a long way. I have been walking these seven days.'
>
> 'Walking for sivin days!' said the young gentleman. 'Oh, I see. **Beak's** order, eh? But,' he added, noticing Oliver's look of surprise, 'I suppose you don't know what a beak is, my flash com-pan-i-on?'
>
> Oliver mildly replied, that he had always heard a bird's mouth described by the term in question.
>
> 'My eyes, how green!' exclaimed the young gentleman.

snub-nosed: button-nosed

roystering: boisterous

bluchers: strong leather half-boots with a high heel

beak: magistrate/judge

Tasks

1 What does Dodger's appearance suggest about him and his lifestyle?
2 What do his actions and behaviours suggest about him?
3 What can you infer from the way he speaks?
4 What do you learn about Dodger and Oliver from their brief interaction?

The writer provides a detailed description but he intends for the reader to form their own impressions about the character; for example, we acknowledge Dodger is a character of contradiction as he is described as 'juvenile' but dresses like a man. He is referred to as a 'young gentleman' but speaks in a common voice. He speaks using exclamations which suggest he is a more confident character than Oliver who speaks 'mildly'.

It is often better to describe rather than 'tell' the reader what a character is like. By implying or suggesting ideas, the reader is able to make their own judgements and form their own impressions.

> **Typical mistake**
>
> Students' responses often lack focus. Be selective about what aspects of character you want to prioritise. Details shared with the reader should enhance the characterisation.

Task

The extract below has been taken from a GCSE student's response. In it they describe a character:

> Don Stefano was a gangster. He had a round face, black hair and dark eyes. He dressed in sharp suits and always wore a fedora hat. He had a scar on his right brow after an incident which took place about fifteen years ago. He was especially proud of his black moustache, which was thick and curled at the ends. He had black beady eyes which frightened anyone who dared look at him.

Mark scheme

Level 1	Limited development of ideas with simple descriptions and few language techniques.
	Simple awareness of purpose, audience and form.
Level 2	Some successful communication and development of ideas with attempts to use language techniques which are fitting for audience and purpose.
	Sensible organisation of ideas which, in places, might be linked by structural features.
Level 3	Mostly successful communication and development of original ideas and descriptions.
	Uses language techniques with increasing success to gain the interest of the audience.
	Successful organisation of ideas with clear evidence of structural features.
Level 4	Communicates and develops ideas in a way that is original and convincing.
	Successfully uses a variety of language techniques throughout the response to enhance the engagement of the reader.
	Skilful organisation of ideas.
Level 5	Highly confident development of ideas in a style which is highly engaging and successfully hooks and holds the reader's interest.
	Confidently employs a full range of language techniques which are used precisely to make the writing original and compelling.
	Assured organisation of ideas with structural features.

Read the improved version below and the comments which indicate what the student has done well.

The place was brimming with criminals in those days but in New York every cop quaked in their boots at the very mention of the name 'Don Stefano'.

The man was lean and slippery. His face was round and full like a stone boulder. On top of his head sat a layer of thick raven-black hair, slicked back with heaps of gel. Unlike the top of his head, the sides were clean shaven, so sharply that you'd cut your palm if you ran your hand across them. His personal barber must have been a surgeon with a razor to cut hair so finely and precisely without slicing through the bulging blue veins behind each ear.

Stefano always wore a fedora hat which leaned slightly to the right so it concealed his right brow. It was where his scar was, the scar that proved he was in fact human. He had sustained it in a late-night shoot-out about fifteen years ago and he'd never got used to the blemish on his face. He never got comfortable with the fact he had been so close to death.

Stefano sported the most masterful of moustaches under his short stumpy nose. Like his hair on top, it was a black bush on his upper lip, but craftily curled at the ends. During his pensive moments, he would tease the ends of the moustache through his lean fingers, tightly coiling it round with each dark thought. Then he'd release a finger and let it spring back onto his cheek, elaborately curled like a snail's shell.

Don Stefano had been graced with a harsh face, hardened by crime and made arrogant by reputation. His black beady eyes never betrayed him; they forever looked sinister and menacing.

Stefano was one dapper criminal, you had to give him that; he was the type of man who made choosing an outfit an art form.

Opening sentence establishes how others regard this character

Simile

Adjectives

Description is developed

Physical description reveals aspects of the character's personality and his past

Alliteration

Physical description is used to reveal character's actions and behaviours

Each paragraph focuses on another physical feature to gradually reveal the character

Ideas are implied so the reader can make their own judgements – this is a character who cares about his image

Test yourself

Write a creative story involving this character:

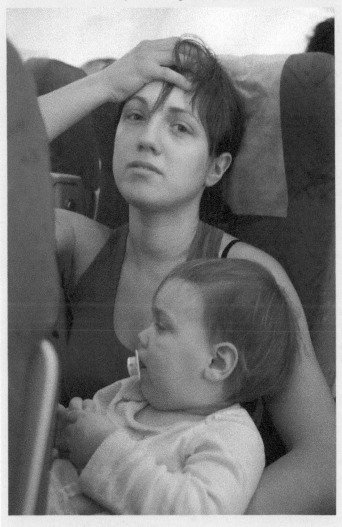

Answers on pp. 94–95

Creating setting

Characters come to life when they are placed within specific settings. When describing a setting you might find it helpful to:
- study the image carefully and think about the sensory response of the character – what can they see; hear; taste; smell and touch?
- don't limit yourself to what is shown in the image – think about how the setting changes as the character will journey through this place
- consider the character's thoughts and feelings towards the setting.

It is important that your writing is a response to the given image so if it shows a setting then keep the location as your focus, avoid drifting off into a character-based narration and keep the reader's attention on the setting and the events which unfold there.

Help yourself by:
- planning thoroughly
- crafting an effective opening and ending

> **Exam tip**
>
> Successful writers will blend elements of each of these approaches into their writing.

- including features to engage the reader – you should try to use:
  - sensory details
  - figurative language – simile, metaphor, alliteration, personification and onomatopoeia
  - a rich and varied vocabulary – think carefully about your choice of verbs, adverbs and adjectives
  - moments of dialogue
  - contrast.

Tasks

Consider the contrast in effectiveness in each of these sentences:

Original	Improved
The room was extremely untidy.	The room was a scene of disorder and abandonment; there were clothes littered everywhere, the bed was unmade; the curtains torn and faded and the bins were overflowing with rubbish. The furniture was covered in a layer of silver dust and a musty smell made the entire place unwelcoming.
Before me stood tall trees.	Like giant guardians, a line of trees stood tall and proud on either side of the gravel pathway which snaked its way through the forest.
The girl walked through the snow.	Gingerly, the girl made her way up the snow-covered path, grateful that she would soon be enjoying the comfort of a blazing fire.

1 Add sensory details to make these descriptions more interesting and vivid:
  (a) Opening the door, I first noticed…
  (b) The weather that day was…
2 Add figurative language to complete these sentences. Be original:
  (a) Like … (simile), the old house was crumbling.
  (b) … (alliteration) and …ing (onomatopoeia) the children raced towards the party table.
  (c) The rain (metaphor), (metaphorical verb) …ing against the windows of the old cottage.
3 Add dramatic verbs, adjectives and adverbs to these sentences:
  (a) At the sound of the bell, the students (verb) out of the classroom and (verb) down the corridor.
  (b) A figure, … and … (adjectives), could be seen in the upstairs window.
  (c) (adverb) the crowds (verb) into the concert hall.

This description has been taken from a famous novel, *Brideshead Revisited* by Evelyn Waugh:

Outside the hut I stood bemused. The rain had ceased but the clouds hung low and heavy overhead. It was a still morning and the smoke from the cookhouse rose straight to the leaden sky. A cart-track, once metalled, then overgrown, now **rutted** and churned to mud, followed the contour of the hillside and dipped out of sight below a **knoll**, and on either side of it lay the haphazard litter of corrugated iron, from which rose the rattle and chatter and whistling and catcalls, all the zoo-noises of the battalion beginning a new day.

Character is used to offer a description of the setting

Precise vocabulary: well-chosen verbs and adjective

Vivid adjective

Detailed description which contrasts how the path was with how it now appears

Precise choice of adjective

Onomatopoeia

Overly long sentence to convey richness of the setting – lots of sights and sounds to absorb.

rutted: bumpy and uneven

knoll: a small rounded hill

Task

Read the Level 3 response below. Try to make it more vivid and interesting by including:

- better verbs, and some adjectives and adverbs
- at least one simile, one metaphor, one use of alliteration and possibly one instance of personification
- description based on the senses
- extra detail
- a variation of sentence lengths for impact.

> The old church was covered in moss. The stained-glass windows were dirty and the lock on the door was rusted. It had once been a beautiful place with beautiful gardens. Now the garden was full of weeds with only an occasional flower sticking out to show there were still some signs of life and beauty about the place. In the far corner of the grounds I could see an old tree, it was the same tree where I had once carved my name as a small child when I enjoyed playing in this place. Carefully, I made my way over, trying to avoid the thorny leaves. I pulled back the heavy branches of the tree and looked to see if my carving was still there.

Test yourself

TESTED

Using all you have learned about bringing settings to life, write a creative story set in this location:

Answers on pp. 94–95

Creating atmosphere

REVISED

Crafting a successful description depends upon well-chosen images and establishing an appropriate **atmosphere**. Creating atmosphere requires you to think carefully about your language choices and your sentence structuring.

> **atmosphere:** the mood or feeling of a piece of writing

Tasks

Below is a famous extract from *The Woman in Black*, in which the writer, Susan Hill, is describing the fog. Read it carefully.

> Fog was outdoors, hanging over the river, creeping in and out of alleyways and passages, swirling thickly between bare trees of all

Pleasant = delightful
Claustrophobic = Suffocating

the parks and gardens of the city, and indoors too, seething through cracks and crannies like sour breath, gaining a sly entrance at every opening of a door. It was a yellow fog, a filthy, evil-smelling fog, a fog that choked and blinded, smeared and stained. Groping their way blindly across roads, men and women took their lives in their hands, stumbling along the pavements, they clutched at railings and at one another, for guidance.

1 Identify the words which best describe the atmosphere created by the writer:
  ○ pleasant   ○ claustrophobic   ○ unsettling   ○ tranquil
  ○ gloomy   ○ oppressive   ○ ominous   ○ cheerful
2 Highlight the **verbs** and **adjectives** used by the writer.
3 Highlight other words and phrases which help create the atmosphere. Explain their effect.

Read one student's response below.

> I stepped into the hallway and stopped to listen. I could only hear my own breathing but I was certain I wasn't alone. Inside was dark, like the sun had completely disappeared or refused to shine on this place. I walked forwards towards the staircase. The dust was thick and the place was covered in cobwebs, it was difficult not to choke. I didn't want to alert anyone to my intrusion. Holding the handrail, I climbed the stairs, wondering if I would make it out again.

The student has tried to create a tense atmosphere but it could be improved by:
● including dramatic verbs, adjectives and adverbs
● including a **simile** or **metaphor**
● changing the sentence structures to include a greater variety of sentence lengths.

Tasks

1 Rewrite the student's response above, including some of the suggested improvements, to increase the tension within the piece of writing.
2 Study the image below:

Write a few paragraphs about this setting. Think carefully about the atmosphere you want to create. Make careful decisions about your choice of verbs, adjectives, adverbs, similes and metaphors.

---

verbs: action words

adjectives: descriptive words

---

simile: a comparison of two things using 'like' or 'as'; for example, 'Like wild animals, the children attacked the plates of sweets and cakes'

metaphor: a comparison of two things using 'is' or 'was'; for example, 'The teacher was a dragon'

Exam tip

Short sentences can be an effective way of adding tension.

Crafting for effect

When writing is being assessed, you should be aware that your response will attract 2 marks: 1 for content and 1 for accuracy. As up to 30 marks are available for producing an accurate response which uses a variety of sentence types and vocabulary for effect, it is advised that you spend ten minutes reading over your work to check for accuracy and opportunities to edit for improvement.

The examiner is looking for a response in which:
- basic spelling, punctuation and grammar are accurate
- there is a deliberate attempt to use more ambitious vocabulary
- a range of sentence types and sentence structures have been used
- there is a deliberate attempt to use more ambitious punctuation to enhance meaning.

Task

Below is a student-friendly mark scheme for spelling, punctuation, grammar, vocabulary and sentence structures. Read it carefully and identify the skills you need to focus on to secure the upper levels.

Mark scheme

Level 3	Some variation in sentence structures.
	Accurate use of full stops, commas, question marks and exclamation marks with some evidence of punctuation deliberately used to add impact.
	Attempts to use a wide and varied vocabulary, including some ambitious words.
Level 4	Evidence of deliberate variation in sentence structures to enhance meaning.
	Successfully employs a range of punctuation throughout the response.
	Accurate spelling, with only occasional errors in the use of challenging words.
	Evidence of a precise and varied vocabulary.
Level 5	A full range of sentence structures are used to enhance the overall response.
	Confidently uses a full range of punctuation.
	Virtually all spellings are accurate with only one-off errors which are likely to occur as an attempt to use more ambitious and complex language.
	Evidence of sophisticated vocabulary.

Sentence structures

Using a range of sentence types and sentence lengths will help you communicate your ideas more effectively as they allow you to:
- emphasise certain points
- speed up or slow down the pace of the writing
- create a desired atmosphere
- give detail or leave an impression upon the reader.

Furthermore, being able to employ a range of sentence types and lengths shows the examiner you are a writer who crafts their response with consideration of the reader.

Sentence types

As you discovered in Unit 1, Section A, you should use different sentence types. If you need to, go back and review the difference between **simple**, **compound** and **complex** sentences.

This is an example from a creative response:

> The ground was uneven. The path had all but disappeared and I was beginning to doubt my own sense of direction. The entire place was silent, except for the cawing of the birds overhead who seemed to share my feeling of uneasiness. I had to keep going. Suddenly, the whole place seemed to darken and close in on me as the moon disappeared below the treetops, leaving me feeling completely isolated. It would soon be pitch black, but I remained hopeful.

simple sentence
compound sentence
complex sentence
simple sentence
complex sentence
compound sentence

Task

Write a short paragraph describing a visit to your school at night time. Consider:

- beginning with a simple sentence
- ending with a compound sentence
- including at least two complex sentences.

> **Exam tip**
>
> When checking through your work, look for a variety of sentence types within your response.

Sentence lengths

As well as using a range of sentence types, you should use long and short sentences to enhance your writing.

Read this extract below taken from *The Mill on the Floss* by George Eliot. The character Maggie has forgotten to feed her brother Tom's rabbits whilst he has been away at boarding school and they have died. Maggie is nervous about revealing the truth to Tom:

> Maggie's heart began to flutter with fear. She dared not tell the sad truth at once, but she walked after Tom in trembling silence as he went out, thinking how she could tell him the news so as to soften at once his sorrow and his anger; for Maggie dreaded Tom's anger of all things; it was quite a different anger from her own.
>
> 'Oh, but, Tom, they're all dead.'
>
> ...Tom stopped immediately in his walk and turned round toward Maggie. 'You forgot to feed 'em, then, and Harry forgot?' he said, his colour heightening for a moment, but soon subsiding. 'I'll pitch into Harry. I'll have him turned away. And I don't love you, Maggie. You sha'n't go fishing with me to-morrow. I told you to go and see the rabbits every day.' He walked on again.

Short sentence to create an atmosphere of tension and emphasise Maggie's unease.

Overly long sentence to reflect Maggie's growing fear and anxiety.

Short sentence for Maggie's dramatic confession.

Long, complex sentence as Tom tries to process what has happened.

Three short simple sentences to reflect the tension and emphasise Tom's anger.

Short simple sentence to end the extract on a tense atmosphere with the conflict unresolved.

Task

Imagine a scene where one character makes a revelation to another. Write a short paragraph, using a variety of sentence types and sentence lengths to create atmosphere, and convey the emotions of the characters involved.

Vocabulary for effect

Part of your writing mark is based on your ability to use language for effect. This includes the quality and variation of vocabulary as well as the quality of your expression. In an examination, you are expected to write in Standard English and demonstrate an ability to use a wide and precise vocabulary.

The examiner is looking for a response that:
- is written in correct Standard English
- uses an appropriate but ambitious vocabulary
- communicates ideas in a way that is original and interesting.

> **Exam tip**
>
> Aim to impress your examiner by taking risks with your vocabulary. Don't settle for the first word that comes to mind just because you know how to spell it. An examiner will prefer to see that you have attempted to use a wide vocabulary, even if the spelling is not always accurate.

Making selections of verbs, adverbs and adjectives

REVISED

Using a good range of vocabulary will allow you to express yourself much more confidently and clearly.

> **Exam tip**
>
> In preparation for the exam, keep a record of vocabulary which impresses you and which you will try to use in your own writing.

Task

Using a thesaurus, find two **synonyms** and two **antonyms** for each of these words:

- said
- walked
- nice
- sad
- happy
- angry
- carefully
- slowly
- quickly

synonym: a word or phrase which means the same or almost the same as another word

antonym: a word that is opposite in meaning to another

Well-chosen adjectives and verbs can make a difference to your writing but the real skill comes from knowing when to use them. Placing an adjective in front of every noun or an adverb alongside every verb will make your writing seem contrived and predictable.

Task

Read the following unimaginative description. Improve it by replacing some of the vocabulary and changing the sentences:

> The woman was really beautiful. I couldn't take my eyes off her magnificent dress and her twinkling blue eyes. She didn't know just how beautiful she was as she walked elegantly across the thick blue carpet and stood on the wooden dance floor, waiting for the talented musicians to begin. When the melodic music commenced she danced enthusiastically, clearly enjoying every minute. Quietly I stood in the corner by the old oak table unable to take my eyes off her. She was gorgeous. I had to have her.

Adjectives can influence a reader's response as they are often categorised as 'positive' or 'negative'.

> **Exam tip**
>
> Do not get concerned about using 'big' words, instead concentrate on using the best words.

> **Exam tip**
>
> Try to use verbs which give an indication of feeling. 'Walked' tells the reader a character put one foot in front of the other, whereas 'marched' implies someone moving with intent.

Tasks

1 Look at the following list of adjectives and decide whether they are positive or negative. You should use a dictionary to look up any words you do not know:

○ laborious   ○ jubilant   ○ salubrious
○ exhilarating   ○ despondent   ○ depraved
○ lurid   ○ tedious   ○ benevolent
○ hostile   ○ opulent

2 Now think of five ambitious adjectives to describe a beautiful hotel.

Describing feelings

In both Personal and Creative Writing, the reader is interested in the reactions and feelings of the people and characters involved. To do this successfully, you should:

● describe, don't tell – describe how certain feelings and emotions manifest themselves in outward appearances and actions; for example, nervousness might cause blushing or fidgeting with restless eyes that look downwards

● think about how a feeling begins and how it grows; for example, unease might escalate to fear which could increase to terror.

> **Typical mistake**
>
> Students can sometimes fail to realise there is a spectrum of emotions and lack the vocabulary to accurately describe what they are feeling. A lot of students will state they are 'afraid' then they become 'really afraid' – this is not a precise use of vocabulary.

Tasks

1 Take each of these emotions and find words to describe the emotion as it intensifies:

(a) contentment   (c) frustration
(b) upset   (d) glum

2 Write a short paragraph about opening a present which failed to impress you. Capture the changing feelings from excitement to disappointment. Be precise with your language choices and use a variety of sentence types and lengths to enhance your writing.

Imagery

Imagery enriches your descriptive writing and adds interest. Similes and metaphors can be effective in helping your reader to conjure up vivid mental images.

Tasks

In the extract taken from *I Know Why the Caged Bird Sings* by Maya Angelou, the narrator is describing her brother:

> His hair fell down in black curls, and my head was covered with black steel wool. And yet he loved me ...When our elders said unkind things about my features (my family was handsome to a point of pain for me), Bailey would wink at me from across the room, and I knew that it was a matter of time before he would take revenge. He would allow the old ladies to finish wondering how on earth I came about, then he would ask, in a voice like cooling bacon grease, 'Oh Miztriz Coleman, how is your son? I saw him the other day, and he looked sick enough to die.'

— metaphor ("black steel wool")
— simile ("cooling bacon grease")

After our early chores were done, while Uncle Willie or Momma minded the Store, we were free to play the children's games as long as we stayed within yelling distance ... In follow the leader, naturally he was the one who created the most daring and interesting things to do. And when he was on the tail of pop the whip, he would twirl off the end like a top, spinning, falling, laughing, finally stopping just before my heart beat its last, and then he was back in the game, still laughing. ←———simile

1 What image of her hair does the writer create through her choice of metaphor?

2 What does the first simile tell the reader about how the writer's brother Bailey speaks to the old women?

3 The second simile is well placed to build upon the impression of Bailey as a character who generates fun and excitement. What image does it create? How do the verbs which follow it enhance the simile?

4 Write a short description about a young child waking up on Christmas morning. Try to convey their feelings and include:
   ○ two or three metaphors
   ○ one or two similes.

Personification can also be used as a method of describing something so that your reader can **vividly** imagine it.

The extract below has been taken from a famous short story, 'The Red Room' by H.G. Wells. The writer has used personification to emphasise the atmosphere of fear and tension.

The long, draughty, **subterranean** passage was chilly and dusty, and my candle flared and **made the shadows cower and quiver**. The echoes rang up and down the spiral staircase, and **a shadow came sweeping up after me**, and one **fled before me** into the darkness overhead. I came along the landing and stopped there for a moment, listening to a rustling sound that I fancied I heard; then, satisfied of the absolute silence, I pushed open the ... door and stood in the corridor.

Tasks

1 Imagine you are writing about walking home in a snowstorm. Write a six-sentence paragraph which includes two uses of personification.

2 Write the opening paragraph where you describe you or a fictional character sitting in front of a fire on a winter's night. Make sure vary your sentence types and use:
   ○ powerful verbs, adjectives and adverbs
   ○ imagery – similes, metaphors and personification.

Exam tip

Create original similes and metaphors.

---

personification: describing a non-living thing as though it were human

vividly: in a way that creates clear images in the mind of the reader

---

subterranean: underground

Exam tip

Choose your verbs very carefully when creating personification.

Typical mistakes

Students often:
● overuse adjectives
● use clichéd similes and metaphors
● forget to use imagery.

Test yourself

Using what you have learned, answer either the Personal or Creative Writing task below:

Write a personal essay for the examiner about a time you made a discovery.

OR

Write a creative response for the examiner. Your writing should be based on the image below. Give your work a suitable title.

Answers on pp. 94–95

How to prepare for the exam

In order to produce interesting Personal and Creative Writing you must read widely. The more exposure you have to examples of descriptive and interesting writing, the better your own writing will become. Read from biographies and autobiographies to see how personal experiences have been recounted in an interesting and authentic way. If you come across something you like – an unfamiliar word, an expression, a metaphor or a description – write it down and try to adapt it and weave it into your next piece of writing. Reading passages from prose fiction will help you appreciate how writers craft a narrative in a way that interests the reader. Ask your teacher or school librarian to direct you towards suitable texts.

Make sure you are using vocabulary correctly, always look up unfamiliar vocabulary to record the definition and try to write the word in a sentence of your own. Aim to produce a personal vocabulary list or dictionary you can use when practising at home or in class.

Writing is a craft; you must work at it, so practise writing tasks at home and use the student-friendly mark schemes in this section to help you identify the level you are working at. Review tasks that your teacher has assessed and identify your strengths and weaknesses so you know what you need to work on.

What does Unit 4, Section B involve?

What is being assessed?

Section B is assessing your reading skills. This means you are being assessed on your ability to analyse how writers craft their texts to achieve a specific purpose and make an impression upon a reader.

How long do you have?

You have 50 minutes in which to complete three tasks. There will be advice on how long you should spend on each question – follow this advice.

How many marks are available?

The total number of marks available in Unit 4, Section B is 62.

What will the questions ask?

There are three tasks to complete in Section B (Tasks 2–4).

Task 2	32 marks	26 mins	You will have to read two extracts from literary prose texts and compare and contrast how the writers achieve a particular effect. You may be asked to compare and contrast how characters, settings or atmosphere have been created.
Task 3	15 marks	12 mins	You will have to read an extract from a non-fiction text and analyse the writer's craft, showing appreciation of how they engage a reader.
Task 4	15 marks	12 mins	You will have to read an extract from a non-fiction text and analyse the writer's craft, showing appreciation of how they engage a reader.

Exam tip

Tasks 3 and 4 will be based on extracts taken from the same text. Task 3 might be based on the beginning of the text, whereas Task 4 might require you to analyse how the ending has been crafted.

Typical mistake

Students must ensure their response is based only on the identified extract linked to each question.

Task 2: Comparing literary texts

The examiner is looking for a response which shows:
- a detailed and perceptive understanding of how writers create meaning
- confidence in analysing writers' craft
- confidence in comparing and contrasting the writers' methods and their effect upon a reader.

Reading literary texts

REVISED

Being able to analyse is an essential skill at GCSE. You begin to show your ability to analyse when you can identify a **writer's intentions**, consider how these intentions have been achieved within the text and explain the effect upon the reader.

> **Exam tip**
>
> In Unit 4, Section B your analysis will be based around linguistic and structural features.

writer's intentions: the effect a writer hopes to achieve or the impression they want to convey through their use of linguistic, structural or presentational features

To develop your analytical skills, you should begin to ask questions as you read through a text.

Task

Read the extract below from *Great Expectations* by Charles Dickens. Answer the questions around the text to help you consider how Dickens presents the character of Magwitch.

What is the effect of introducing this character through his voice?

What impression do we have of the character speaking, based on this adjective?

Text A

'Hold your noise!' cried a terrible voice, as a man started up from among the graves at the side of the church porch. 'Keep still, you little devil, or I'll cut your throat!'

A fearful man, all in coarse grey, with a great iron on his leg. A man with no hat, and with broken shoes, and with an old rag tied round his head. A man who had been soaked in water, and smothered in mud, and lamed by stones, and cut by flints, and stung by nettles, and torn by briars; who limped, and shivered, and glared and growled; and whose teeth chattered in his head as he seized me by the chin.

What does this interaction tell us about the character?

What impression of the man does the writer want us to form based on this description?

What do the different verb choices suggest about the man?

Why might the writer have used a very long sentence here?

Two different students attempted to analyse the above extract from *Great Expectations*. Read their responses:

Student A

The writer of this extract is Charles Dickens. He is writing about a man who is unpleasant and threatening. The writer wants the reader to form a negative impression of the character of Magwitch based on the way he speaks and how he looks. Lots of interesting verbs have been used to help the reader form a clear impression of Magwitch as a character who has been through a lot.

Student B

Immediately the writer encourages his reader to form a negative impression of the character of Magwitch. Dickens decides to introduce the character through dialogue to make his appearance seem unexpected and alarming. The reader imagines a threatening and confident character as he orders, 'Hold your noise!' with the exclamation mark reinforcing his demanding tone. Even his voice is described as 'terrible' and this negative adjective increases our unpleasant impression of the character. His interaction confirms he is dangerous as he claims he will 'cut your throat!' The writer again adds an exclamation mark to emphasise the character's assertive and threatening tone. Through the description of the character, Dickens makes us think of a criminal as he is 'all in coarse grey' like a uniform and he has a 'great iron on his leg' which makes us curious as we infer he is an escaped convict. This awareness only furthers our impression of him as a dangerous and intimidating character. The writer uses lots of verbs to convey the challenges Magwitch has gone through to escape captivity. Verbs such as 'smothered', 'cut' and 'stung' confirm he has encountered struggles but towards the end of the last sentence verbs such as 'limped', 'shivered' and 'chattered' make him seem weak and vulnerable. The final sentence is extremely long and full of dramatic verbs to force the reader to appreciate Magwitch's recent challenges and his desperation to be a free man.

Assessment comment

Student A has a simple understanding of the writer's intentions and the reader's impression of the character. They state **what** their impression is but they are not analysing as they fail to explain how this impression is formed. They do recognise the writer's use of verbs but they fail to quote specific examples or offer a precise explanation of their effect.

Assessment comment

Student B is analysing as they are able to identify **what** decisions the writer has made in crafting the character of Magwitch and **how** his choices have influenced the reader's impression of the character. They quote specific examples from the text and explain their effect. They can comment on language choices and structural features such as the decision to introduce the character through dialogue and the use of a long sentence to end.

Task

Read the extract below. Compose a question which could be asked at each highlighted point to encourage a GCSE student to think about how the writer makes the character of Aunt Lucy seem like a caring character:

Text B

'Hey handsome, let's mop up those tears.' She jerked my chin up so our eyes met. Her green eyes shone like precious jewels and she held my gaze just long enough to reassure me that I was safe. She winked and smiled as she saw me blush. Her warm hands cupped my cheeks and she squeezed them gently before planting her glossy red lips on my forehead. Playfully, she tousled my hair and traced a perfectly manicured finger down the length of my nose, making me feel like I was six years old. Making me feel safe. 'Aunt Lucy's here now,' she soothed.

Comparing texts

REVISED

Comparison is a key element of Task 2. You should have a clear approach for dealing with two texts. Identify the key terms within the question which will identify what you should focus on as you read.

Consider:

- highlighting as you read to identify where the writer uses linguistic or structural features
- annotating briefly to record your observations and reactions to the text.

Exam tip

Annotation should be brief, it is intended to help you and is not for the attention of the examiner so use abbreviations; for example, ' DrVb' for 'dramatic verb', 'met' for 'metaphor' or 'Rdr' for 'reader'.

- starting to think about similarities and differences – begin identifying the ideas communicated by each writer and then think about **how** these ideas are communicated; you can write about Text A and then write about Text B, but identify points of comparison and contrast with Text A as they occur.

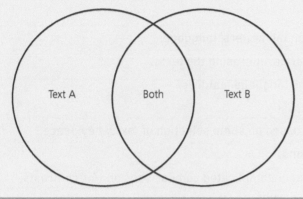

Text A Both Text B

What to look for when comparing and contrasting

When comparing and contrasting you could consider the following:

- How each writer begins their text; for example, a text might open dramatically or descriptively. A writer might favour dialogue to present a character.
- How they conclude their text; for example, a text might end with a resolved or unresolved conclusion. The ending could be predictable or climactic.
- What thoughts or feelings each text induces within a reader and how this is achieved.
- Words or phrases which leave an impression upon a reader – look carefully at the writers' choice of verbs, adjectives and adverbs.
- Language techniques which are used by each writer and their intended effect – remember two writers can achieve a similar effect but use a different technique; for example, one might use a simile whereas the other might use a metaphor.
- How each writer uses sentence types, sentence lengths and punctuation to enhance meaning; for example, sentence lengths can be used to convey emotion such as anger or excitement. They can also create atmosphere such as tension or unease. Punctuation can also emphasise ideas and emotions.
- How the reader's impression or understanding changes as the text develops – do your expectations change as you read through the text? As you read, note when and how these changes occur.

Tasks

1 Look back at the extract from *Great Expectations* and the 'Aunt Lucy' extract. Using a diagram, record ideas and observations to help you answer the task:

Compare and contrast how the writers of Text A (*Great Expectations*) and Text B ('Aunt Lucy') present the adult characters.

Mark scheme

Level 1	Makes simple comments on the writers' language.
	May be reliant on copying or paraphrasing the texts.
	Some awareness of obvious language features.
	May not compare and contrast.
Level 2	Offers general comments based on some selection of textual evidence.
	Straightforward explanations.
	Some success in identifying uncomplicated comparisons and/or contrasts.
Level 3	Offers an appropriate interpretation of the writers' ideas supported by comments on language.
	Generally relevant explanations and selection of evidence from both texts.
	Appropriate comparing and contrasting.
Level 4	Clear understanding of both texts with interpretations supported by examination of language.
	A range of relevant explanations which evaluate the writers' craft.
	A range of relevant evidence selected from both texts for the purpose of effective comparing and contrasting.
Level 5	Confident understanding of both texts with evaluative explanations which show assured appreciation of the intended effect.
	An assured selection of precise evidence from both texts to support skilful comparing and contrasting and precise analysis of writer's craft.

2 Below is the beginning of one student's response, comparing and contrasting how the characters of Magwitch and Aunt Lucy have been depicted. Read carefully and, using the mark scheme above, identify what level this student is working at.

> Both writers introduce their characters through dialogue. In Text A Magwitch speaks using the imperative 'Hold your voice!' and the adjective 'terrible' is added to encourage the reader to form a negative first impression. In contrast, Aunt Lucy's dialogue reveals a character who is complimentary and compassionate. 'Hey handsome, let's mop up those tears.' The word 'hey' is informal, giving the reader the impression she is a character who speaks in a calm and caring tone, unlike Magwitch who speaks in a threatening tone.

— appreciation of writer's craft

— effective comparing and contrasting

— impact upon the reader

3 Use the planning notes below to write two more paragraphs comparing how the characters of Magwitch and Aunt Lucy have been depicted.

Text A (Magwitch): unnamed and repeatedly referred to as 'a man' to increase mystery; unpleasant physical description; negative adjectives; threatening and exclamatory tone; dramatic verbs; long sentence used to end extract.

Both: introduced through dialogue; interactions reveal aspect of character; physical descriptions reveal aspect of character; verb choices reveal aspect of character.

Text B (Aunt Lucy): simile to create positive impression; verbs confirm her calm and kind personality; positive adjectives and adverbs; short sentences used to end extract.

Language to compare and contrast

REVISED

When answering Task 2, you will need to use words and phrases to signpost to the examiner that you are cross-referencing and identifying points of comparison and contrast.

Exam tip

Useful phrases include the following:
- Similarities: both; likewise; also; similarly; in comparison.
- Differences: in contrast; whereas; unlike; although; dissimilar.

Test yourself

TESTED

Read the two extracts below and write a full response to the task:

Text A

I'm running. My chest is tight and sore. Breath rasping and whistling in my lungs. Branches whip against my face. Brambles tear at my legs and arms. There is a voice screaming. Out loud. The sound ripping through the trees, screaming and screaming.

It's my voice.

'Amy! Amy!'

Now I'm at the back dyke and the solid wooden fencing has been torn aside. Blasted apart as if some careless giant had passed by and trodden on it. I stare at the wood, not splintered or broken, but melted. Dissolved and warped. Curled aside to make a small space. Space enough for a child to walk through. What could do that? What power is there that would leave that mark? I hesitate, feeling the first great lurch of fear for myself.

'Amy?' I cry out.

Beyond me the gaping dark of the cemetery.

From Whispers in the Graveyard by Theresa Breslin

Text B

Brian had to get the headset from the pilot. Had to reach over and get the headset from the pilot or he would not be able to use the radio to call for help. He had to reach over...

His hands began trembling again. He did not want to touch the pilot, did not want to reach for him. But he had to. Had to get the radio. He lifted his hands from the wheel, just slightly, and held them waiting to see what would happen. The plane flew on normally, smoothly.

All right, he thought. Now. Now to do this thing. He turned and reached for the headset, slid it from the pilot's head, one eye on the plane, waiting for it to dive. The headset came easily, but the microphone switch at the pilot's belt was jammed in and he had to pull to get it loose. When he pulled, his elbow bumped the wheel and pushed it in and the plane started down in a shallow dive. Brian grabbed the wheel and pulled it back, too hard again, and the plane went through another series of stomach-wrenching swoops up and down before he could get it under control.

From *Hatchett* by Gary Paulsen

Compare and contrast how the writers of Text A and Text B create an atmosphere of tension. Present supporting evidence from both texts.

Answers on pp. 95–96

How to prepare for the exam

Read a range of texts and, as you read, highlight and annotate so you recognise and understand how writers create meaning by using linguistic and structural features.

Find two texts which have something in common in that each might be a description of a setting or a character. They might share a common theme or depict a dramatic experience. Annotate, identify points of comparison and contrast and write up your response in full, remembering to use comparative connectives.

Compare your responses against the mark scheme and evaluate your strengths and weaknesses.

Tasks 3 and 4: Reading non-fiction texts

Tasks 3 and 4 are based on your reading of non-fiction texts. The examiner wants to see that you can:

- understand the writer's intentions
- identify how the writer uses a range of linguistic and structural features
- carefully select a range of appropriate evidence from the text
- comment on textual evidence by explaining the impact upon a reader.

As you read the texts you should consider:

- what is said – the content of the text
- how the text is written – comment on language choices, techniques, sentence structures and tone.

Exam tip

Questions which require you to analyse a writer's craft often contain the word 'how'; for example, 'Explain how the writer...', 'How does the writer...' or 'Consider how the writer...'

Understanding writers' attitudes and intentions

REVISED

Whilst non-fiction texts are based on the real world, they are not always factual or true. In Unit 4, the non-fiction texts often involve a writer promoting a strong point of view or sharing an experience, so they can be **subjective** and **anecdotal** but also highly entertaining.

As in Unit 1, Section B, when you read these texts, you should be aware of explicit meaning and meaning that is implied by the writer. To reach the higher mark levels, you should be able to show an appreciation of the writer's attitudes and implicit meanings within the text.

subjective: based on or influenced by personal feelings or opinions

anecdotal: based on personal accounts and experiences

Mark scheme

Level 1	Simple understanding of the text and its explicit meanings.
	May include some relevant textual evidence.
	Simple comments which might remark on how they achieve effect.
Level 2	Some understanding of the text and the writer's intentions.
	Efforts to select some relevant textual evidence with some general explanation of the effect.
Level 3	General understanding of the text and how the writer's intentions have been communicated explicitly and implicitly through language choices.
	Will include some relevant supporting evidence with explanations which consider effect.
Level 4	Secure understanding of the text and clear recognition of how the writer's intentions are reflected explicitly and implicitly through language choices.
	A secure evaluation of writer's craft which explores aspects of language and structural features by commenting on their impact upon a reader.
Level 5	Confident understanding of the text with precise selection of textual evidence.
	A confident analysis which shows an ability to infer and offer accurate and insightful explanations which consider the writer's intentions and the reader's response.

Tasks

1 Read the extract below where a writer shares her opinion on going to the gym. Consider the questions, which invite you to consider explicit and implicit meaning.

> With a family wedding fast approaching and my waistline ever expanding, I took the desperate step of enrolling in a gym. Big mistake! The only thing shrinking in size was my confidence which diminished by the second as I surveyed the lean, lycra-clad gods and goddesses who had gathered for their daily endorphin fix. Meanwhile, I stood awkwardly tugging at my baggy grey track shorts, wishing I had pasted some false tan onto my bluish-white legs and longing for a packet of crisps. I was an alien! For a moment I considered retreat, but then I caught sight of my muffin top in one of the unforgiving mirrors, made my way to the torturous treadmill and embraced the beginning of my transformation from wobbling woman to fitness freak.

What does the word 'desperate' suggest about the writer's attitude to the gym?

The writer's regret is explicitly stated here but how is it emphasised?

What is the writer implying about the other gym users through this description?

What is implied here about the writer's commitment to weight loss?

What is the writer implying through this metaphor?

What causes the writer to persevere with her gym experience?

2 Read the two sample responses which attempt to answer this question: Explain how the writer conveys her gym experience in a way that engages the reader.

Student A

> The writer has reluctantly joined the gym because she needs to lose weight for a family wedding. She describes her decision as 'desperate' and a 'big mistake.' She feels like she does not belong in the gym and describes how her confidence was 'shrinking' which is rather funny. She thinks the other gym users are attractive and calls them 'gods and goddesses'. She is clearly finding it difficult to commit to losing weight as she is 'longing for a packet of crisps' which again is very humorous. She really wants to leave but catches sight of herself and realises she must stick it out in order to get fit.

Straightforward understanding of explicit meanings

Selects evidence but no explanation or evaluation

Offers a straightforward inference

Straightforward inferences

Reporting instead of analysing

Assessment comment

This response shows an understanding of the text but relies too heavily on explicit meanings. There is some selection of relevant evidence and some implicit understanding. The student understands **what** is communicated but fails to analyse **how** the text is written. This response is typical of low Level 3.

Student B

> It is clear from the beginning that the writer has reluctantly joined the gym as she describes her decision as 'desperate' which implies the pressure of the wedding and her need to lose weight has forced her into this gym membership. She states her regret and emphasises it through a short dramatic sentence, 'Big mistake!' with the exclamation mark reinforcing the fact that she has made a wrong decision. The reader is keen to read on and discover why it has turned out so badly. The writer continues to engage the reader by creating a humorous tone when she states, 'the only thing shrinking was my confidence...' The reader appreciates the humour here in that the aim of visiting the gym was to lose weight and make the writer feel better about herself but it is having a negative impact upon her self-image and self-confidence. She refers to the other gym users as 'gods and goddesses', using exaggeration to create more humour and implying that they looked perfect and not like they needed to visit a gym. This is followed up with 'I was an alien',

Accurate deduction

Appreciates how punctuation enhances meaning

Examples from the text are followed by accurate explanation

a metaphor which forces us to appreciate that the writer is feeling out of place and in the minority which will only increase her feelings of negativity and self-consciousness. An exclamation mark emphasises how unpleasant she felt at this moment, making the reader feel sympathy for her. A long final sentence sees the writer overcome a moment of doubt and reluctance as she makes her way to the 'torturous treadmill' with the adjective 'torturous' implying that she will not enjoy her experience but she accepts it is necessary to achieve her aim. The end is humorous as the reader infers the writer has high expectations as she is hoping for a 'transformation' which will see her turn from 'wobbling woman to fitness freak'. The contrasting alliterative sounds emphasise the change she hopes will take place. The word 'freak' does not have positive connotations and makes the ending humorous as it implies the gym will see her lose weight but might also change her personality, making her obsessed with the gym.

Appreciates implicit meaning and considers the reader's response

Can comment on language and draw inferences

Perceptive analysis of language and appreciation of implicit meaning

Assessment comment

This response makes accurate comments about how the writer communicates ideas and attitudes. The comments on language are analytical and there is evidence of an ability to **infer**. This response is typical of Level 5.

infer: to read between the lines – to arrive at a reasoned conclusion based on what is suggested or implied

Analysing techniques

REVISED ☐

You should now realise that it is not enough to understand what a writer is saying, you must also appreciate **how** they communicate meaning through their language choices and structural features.

Exam tip

Remember: identification + explanation = analysis.

Typical mistake

Many students approach Tasks 3 and 4 as though the aim is to spot techniques. The examiner wants to see that you can analyse and evaluate so you will begin to attract marks when you can explain the impact of the writer's choices upon a reader.

Task

Read the extract below from an article published in the *Telegraph* and the annotations which identify different techniques, words and sentence structures used by the writer.

Why I hate museums ◄————————————————————— opinionated title

Travel guides are filled to the brim with listings for museums and art galleries, each less enticing than the last. After all, it's what sensible, ———— critical tone
sophisticated travellers do. The DK Eyewitness guide to Budapest happens to be on my desk. In its opening 'at a glance' chapter, the very first section is dedicated to the city's 'best' museums and galleries. Forget beautiful parks, trendy bars and historic baths, what tourists ———— 'thrill-a-minute' – sarcastic tone
really want to do – the author believes – is spend an unforgettable hour inside the city's thrill-a-minute Ethnographical Museum. Delve ◄——— alliteration
deeper into the guide and you'll find more obscure but unmissable ———— personal pronoun
'sights', such as the Golden Eagle Pharmacy Museum and the Gizi Bajor Memorial Museum. Who in their right mind wants to spend their precious time off learning about the life and times of a Hungarian ———— rhetorical question
actress?

———— conversational aside

Before stepping inside, ask yourself – and answer honestly – whether this is *really* what you want to do. I had an epiphany on a recent day trip to Florence. A colleague told me that on no account should I leave ———— anecdote
the city without visiting the Uffizi. But when my friend and I arrived

at the gallery, post-lunch, queueing times were estimated at up to 45 minutes. I was torn, but she simply asked: 'What do you *really* feel like doing?' We left the gallery, bought a bottle of red from a nearby deli, pinched a couple of cardboard cups from a cafe, and spent the next few hours slumped by the Arno, enjoying idle conversation while staring wistfully at the Ponte Vecchio. It was wonderful.

— long sentence

— short sentence

Evaluating the effect

REVISED

As in Unit 1, Section B, you will find the Point, Evidence and Explanation (P.E.E.) approach helpful when responding to non-fiction texts. Once you have identified something within a text, you must ensure you can confidently explain and evaluate its impact upon the reader.

Read the sample responses below in which two students have attempted to analyse the museum text.

Student A

> The writer opens the text with a catchy title, 'Why I hate museums'. This makes the reader feel interested and want to read on. Quickly the writer establishes a negative tone with the phrase, 'each less enticing than the last'. The reader recognises this is a highly opinionated piece of writing.

Assessment comment

Student A's response is trying to use P.E.E. but the explanations are general and brief; for example, there is no explanation as to how the title interests a reader. This student could improve by working on their explanations.

Student B

> The writer establishes a negative tone through the title, 'Why I hate museums'. The word 'hate' is rather strong yet succeeds in making the reader intrigued to read on and discover the reasons for this negative attitude as we expect this will be a confessional and subjective piece of writing. The writer's critical tone is furthered when he states, 'each less enticing than the last'. This is of course the writer's opinion, but he has stated it as though it were fact in the hope that he will sway the reader to agree with his strong views.

Exam tip

These phrases will help show the examiner you are beginning to explain and evaluate:
- This confirms...
- The reader infers...
- The effect here is...
- The writer intends...
- This is effective as...
- It is clear that...
- The use of X succeeds in making the reader...

Assessment comment

Student B's response is more analytical as it comments on specific word choices and their impact upon a reader. There is evidence of an appreciation of the writer's attitudes and intentions.

Tasks

1 Look back at the annotated museum text. Select three different features and write an analytical paragraph using P.E.E.
2 Below are the final two paragraphs of the museum text. Read them carefully and produce a list of linguistic and structural features which you can identify in this extract.
Select four features and write an analysis using P.E.E.

> There are some decent museums. I enjoyed a trip to the Old Operating Theatre and Museum in London Bridge; while the Pitts Rivers Museum in Oxford is an undisputed gem. But perhaps that's because I find human organs in pickling jars, trophy scalps and amputation equipment endlessly compelling. Ceramics, on the other hand, are just dull. As is – though this is an opinion that will no doubt upset many, including the colleague who urged me to visit the Uffizi – religious art. On a recent trip to Bruges, I visited the

city's Groeningemuseum. Its collection consisted almost entirely of biblical scenes by Renaissance and Baroque artists. Yes, I have a *very* limited grounding in art history, but to my eye – and to those of many others, I venture – they all looked the same. With each new room I grew more disinterested, and my stride lengthened.

If you want to see tourists shuffling in silence down hospital-like corridors, bored security guards, and jobsworths waiting to pounce on anyone who dares to laugh, send a text message or eat a biscuit, then museums are for you.

From Oliver Smith in *The Telegraph* (19 August 2014)

Test yourself

Read the text below which has been taken from the beginning of an article published in *The Telegraph* in which the writer discusses her selfie obsession.

1 Explain how the writer has tried to engage the interest of the reader.

Generation selfie: Has posing, pouting and posting turned us all into narcissists?

'What on earth were you thinking?' I am looking at my husband's Instagram feed, where a picture of me shivering in a wetsuit stares back at me: hair flat against my face, make-up free, bum blocking the beach. 'I was thinking you looked really happy,' he says, wounded.

As I try to explain why I'm reacting like a celebrity who has just spotted a paparazzo up a tree, how this photo amounts to career suicide, even defamation, I realise that his is, of course, the saner voice. But these days mine is the normal voice. Most women I know would react the same way. In the age of social media and selfies, it's become natural meticulously to police images of ourselves. I've never thought of myself as high-maintenance – I go make-up-free on holidays, can get ready for a night out in under 15 minutes and never expect to look better than passable – yet I know my good angles, I've perfected a selfie-smile and I have preferred Instagram filters. And I'm not the only one. Vanity has exploded on an epic scale.

The extract below is the final two paragraphs of the article.

2 Explain how the writer conveys her selfie obsession as extreme.

When I joined Instagram a year ago I was clueless, convinced nobody wanted to see my holiday snaps or pictures of my breakfast. Within weeks I realised that a) they did and b) they wanted to see the face behind the camera. Soon I'd become adept in the dark arts of the selfie – grinning in a kagoul in an Alpine hut, drinking Guinness in a Belfast bar, waving from a sunlounger in Antigua.

I know my good angles: I've learnt never to lean into a picture (it makes you look crazy), and I'm on my way to adopting a celebrity 'mono-face', like Victoria Beckham's pout or Jennifer Aniston's semi-smile. I've lost any reticence about asking people to take my photograph. Last week I shouted, 'No, don't crouch down – you'll give me a double-chin,' at a New York cop who'd offered to take my picture on Brooklyn Bridge. It's terrifying how quickly I've become comfortable with behaviour that would have struck me as flagrant narcissism a year ago. It's also terrifying that the cop didn't balk – he was clearly used to art direction.

Answers on p.96

How to prepare for the exam

You need practice in annotating, analysing and evaluating texts.

Read and annotate short non-fiction extracts and, as you read, ask questions which encourage you to think about the writer's intentions. For example: What does the writer want me to think or feel as I read? Why might the writer have used this word? What is emphasised through this short sentence?

Practise answering under timed conditions and use the mark schemes to assess your work and gain an understanding of your strengths and weaknesses.

Test yourself answers

Unit 1, Section A

Page 9, Compose an exam question

1 Topic: School uniform
   Purpose: To promote a point of view – to inform, explain and argue
   Audience: Classmates/peers
   Form: Speech
   Sample question: Write a speech to be delivered to your classmates promoting your views on whether or not school uniform should be scrapped.
2 Suggestions to improve the sample response include: adopt a formal register and tone; engage their audience; use a varied vocabulary, rather than rely on 'ugly'; use a variety of sentence lengths and punctuation and avoid starting a sentence with 'And'.
3 Your improved response should be more formal and may include some of the improvements suggested above.

Page 10, Select a task and write an introduction

Your introduction should:
- show an awareness of audience – you may have used direct address; inclusive language; asked a question; welcomed your audience if writing a speech or used an appropriate greeting for a letter or email
- show an awareness of purpose – your introduction should refer to the topic and it should be clear why you are writing
- show an awareness of form – it should be clear from your first few sentences what form your writing is taking
- use an appropriate register and tone – the letter, speech and article should all be written in a formal tone. The blog can be 'chatty' but formal and the email to a friend will be informal.

Page 12, Writing a plan for website article on the stresses of being a teenager

Your plan should include five or six ideas, notes on how each idea will be developed, techniques you will use to strengthen your points and/or engage your reader and numbers to indicate the order in which you will write up each point.

Page 14, Write the opening and concluding paragraphs for a speech to persuade your audience to recycle more

Your writing should show attempts to:
- be assertive and confident when stating your ideas, e.g. 'We all know…' or 'It is a fact that…'
- use inclusive language to engage your reader
- use a variety of sentence lengths, e.g. short, punchy sentences to make confident statements
- use a variety of punctuation, e.g. exclamation marks to convey strong feelings
- use a variety of linguistic techniques, e.g. rhetorical questions, imperatives, triples, humour or exaggeration
- in your introduction, give your reader a flavour of your arguments
- in your conclusion, you should leave an impression upon your reader.

Page 16, Engaging a reader

Write a paragraph in which you argue school trips are too expensive and do not offer value for money.

To engage your reader, you may have included:
- persuasive language (see page 16 for suggestions)
- conversational phrases
- direct address
- inclusive language.

Page 18, Write the opening and concluding paragraphs to a speech to persuade your classmates of the benefits of homework

Your plan should include five or six ideas, notes on how each idea will be developed, techniques you will use to strengthen your points and/or engage your reader and numbers to indicate the order in which you will write up each point.

Your writing should show attempts to:
- be assertive and confident when stating your ideas, e.g. 'We all know…' or 'It is a fact that…'
- use inclusive language to engage your reader
- use a variety of persuasive techniques (remember: *RAINFOREST*)
- use a variety of sentences lengths, e.g. short, punchy sentences to make confident statements
- use a variety of punctuation, e.g. exclamation marks to convey strong feelings
- use a variety of linguistic techniques, e.g. rhetorical questions, imperatives, triples, humour or exaggeration
- in your introduction give your reader a flavour of your arguments
- in your conclusion, you should leave an impression upon your reader.

Page 18, Write an article in which you put forward your views on the topic: 'The internet is addictive and dangerous'

Use the grid below to assess which level you are writing at and then set yourself a target for next time:

Level 1	Limited awareness of audience and purpose.
	Uncomplicated style with simple/few language techniques.
	Limited evidence of structural features.
Level 2	Some awareness of audience and purpose.
	Ideas are developed to promote a point of view or compel the reader.
	Some recognition of form.
	Some successful attempts to use language techniques and structural features.
Level 3	Clear awareness of audience and purpose.
	Ideas are developed in an interesting way with a range of language techniques to engage or compel the reader.
	Writes with a clear appreciation of form.
	Evidence of a variety of structural features.
Level 4	Confident awareness of audience and purpose.
	Ideas are developed in a way that is increasingly convincing and compelling.
	Confident recognition of form.
	Successfully uses a variety of language techniques throughout the response with structural features used to enhance meaning and/or engagement.
Level 5	Highly impressive awareness of audience and purpose.
	Highly confident development of a range of ideas to make the piece engaging and interesting.
	Assured recognition of form.
	Highly confident in using a full range of language techniques to achieve effects.
	Assured organisation of ideas with structural features.

Page 20, Identifying ten errors

1 musicle should be musical
2 benefical should be beneficial
3 manege should be manage
4 reliefer should be reliever
5 oppurtunity should be opportunity
6 stimulite should be stimulate
7 espshially should be especially
8 alot should be a lot (two words)
9 practise (verb) should be practice (noun)
10 affectively should be effectively

Page 21, Write two paragraphs promoting your views on the topic: 'Animal testing is unnecessary and cruel'

Tick where you have shown an ability to:
- write convincingly
- use a variety of techniques to add interest and engage your reader
- make deliberate decisions about vocabulary to influence how your reader thinks and feels as they read your response.

Page 23, Write a paragraph in which you defend sport and modern-day sports stars

Tick in your answer where you have shown an ability to:

- use a variety of sentence types and sentence lengths
- use a variety of linguistic devices
- carefully choose your vocabulary.

Page 24, Write three paragraphs in which you promote the benefits of introducing financial education to the school curriculum

Tick in your answer where you have shown your ability to:

- make accurate use of basic punctuation

- include at least four examples of more ambitious punctuation – brackets; ellipsis; colon; semi-colon or dashes.

Pages 26–29

For all of the following tasks, use the mark schemes that follow to assess how successful your response is.

- Page 26: Write a speech to be delivered to your local council to persuade them to organise a festival for young people.
- Page 27: Plan and write a short article for your local paper in which you promote your concerns about the increasing number of fast-food outlets in the neighbourhood.
- Page 28: Plan and write a letter of your own to your local tourist board about the need for improved tourist attractions in Northern Ireland.
- Page 29: Plan and write an online blog where you promote your views on television talent shows.

Content

Level 1	Limited awareness of audience and purpose.
	Uncomplicated style with simple/few language techniques.
	Limited evidence of structural features.
Level 2	Some awareness of audience and purpose.
	Ideas are developed to promote a point of view or compel the reader.
	Some recognition of form.
	Some successful attempts to use language techniques and structural features.
Level 3	Clear awareness of audience and purpose.
	Ideas are developed in an interesting way with a range of language techniques to engage or compel the reader.
	Writes with a clear appreciation of form.
	Evidence of a variety of structural features.
Level 4	Confident awareness of audience and purpose.
	Ideas are developed in a way that is increasingly convincing and compelling.
	Confident recognition of form.
	Successfully uses a variety of language techniques throughout the response with structural features used to enhance meaning and/or engagement.
Level 5	Highly impressive awareness of audience and purpose.
	Highly confident development of a range of ideas to make the piece engaging and interesting.
	Assured recognition of form.
	Highly confident in using a full range of language techniques to achieve effects.
	Assured organisation of ideas with structural features.

SPG

Level 1	Simple sentence structuring.
	Basic punctuation used with some accuracy.
	Limited vocabulary with some accuracy in spelling of simple words.
Level 2	Straightforward sentence structuring.
	Accurate use of simple punctuation, such as full stops and commas, to achieve straightforward communication.
	Some evidence of vocabulary used to enhance the response with accurate spelling of uncomplicated words.
Level 3	Some variation in sentence structures.
	Accurate use of full stops, commas, question marks and exclamation marks with some evidence of punctuation used to add impact.
	Attempts to use a wide and varied vocabulary with accurate spelling of straightforward words and some more complex words.
Level 4	Deliberate variation in sentence structures.
	Employs a range of punctuation throughout the response to maintain precision in expression and engage the audience.
	Evidence of a precise and varied vocabulary with only occasional errors in the use of challenging words.
Level 5	A full range of sentence structures are used.
	Confidently uses a full range of punctuation.
	Evidence of sophisticated vocabulary and virtually all spelling is accurate.

Unit 1, Section B

Page 35, Hudson River text: Explain how the writer emphasises the sense of drama to engage the reader

You may have selected and explained the following:

- Direct speech to emphasise the unexpected announcement from the captain and to convey his urgent tone through the imperative phrase, 'brace for impact'.
- Second sentence is long to reflect the writer's attempts to recall how to respond to this command.
- Confession that she 'had never paid attention to the emergency drill' allows us to infer panic.
- Dramatic language – 'grabbed' and 'held on tightly' – emphasises her helplessness.
- Short dramatic sentence, 'Just in time.'
- Adjectives add impact, 'incredible force'.
- Dramatic verbs – 'hurled' and 'plunged' – convey the force of the impact.
- 'Someone screamed' forces the reader to infer the increasing panic.
- 'We're in water' increases the danger and the reaction of the passengers confirms their

desperation to escape, 'We all jumped to our feet, jostling…'
- Increasing danger with an awareness that the 'back of the plane was submerged…'
- Auditory description of 'people screaming' forces the reader to imagine the horror and panic.
- First person 'I need to get out' emphasises the writer's feelings of isolation – in this moment it was everyone for themselves.
- Description such as 'freezing water' and 'icy wing' continue the atmosphere of danger.
- Sibilant phrase – 'soaking and shivering' – makes the writer seem vulnerable.
- Personification – 'wind howling down the river' – sees the extract end rather ominously.

Page 37, Summarising: Write down two reasons the writer gives to explain his lack of support for the war

- Reason 1: He believes the war could have ceased earlier but people in power wish to continue the conflict to pursue their own aims to gain power and control over others.

○ Evidence 1: 'I believe that the war is being deliberately prolonged by those who have the power to end it.'

○ Evidence 2: 'I believe that this war, upon which I entered as a war of defence and liberation, has now become a war of aggression and conquest.'

● Reason 2: He believes that the lives of soldiers are of little concern to those in power, whom he accuses of poor decision making, and therefore he

can no longer stand by and watch his comrades suffer and die for a cause he does not believe in.

○ Evidence 1: 'I have seen and endured the sufferings of the troops and I can no longer be a party to prolong these sufferings for ends which I believe to be evil and unjust.'

○ Evidence 2: 'I am … protesting against … the political errors and insincerities for which the fighting men are being sacrificed.'

Page 39, Child and mother extract

1 Evidence:

Summary	Evidence
The child and his mother have a strong relationship.	'For the first four years of my life, I had relied upon my mother offering her hand to reassure me, to let me know she was always there and would never leave me.' OR 'I remember busily colouring in a picture for Mum to add to her "gallery" which she proudly displayed on the kitchen walls.'
This event has been a defining moment in the life of the writer.	'I wasn't ready for this act of abandonment.' OR 'On that traumatic September afternoon, everything changed.'
The child feels let down by his mother.	'Mum was leaving me with a complete stranger; it felt like the ultimate betrayal.'
The experience is an emotional one for the child.	'Mum was prising her hand out of my vice-like grip.' OR 'I struggled to make sense of what was happening.' OR 'Mum,' I yelled, holding up my latest masterpiece, so certain it would stop her in her tracks, send her running in my direction to scoop me up and take us both to the park. She didn't look back. She kept on walking.' OR '"Soon." What did that mean? What four-year-old understands the word "soon"?'
The experience is an emotional one for the mother.	'She was smiling but her voice was full of anxiety and her eyes were full of tears.'
The teacher is not a very empathetic individual.	'"Mum will be back soon," said the stranger, smiling, but it wasn't a "Mum" smile; it was the same smile she had for all the other crying kids.' OR '…already she had an eye on the boy throwing sand at the opposite side of the room.'

2 You may have referred to the following:

● Reason 1: It was so memorable because it was the first memory the writer has of being separated from his mother and it was such an unexpected and unpleasant experience.

○ Evidence 1: 'I wasn't ready for this act of abandonment.'

○ Evidence 2: 'For the first four years of my life, I had relied upon my mother offering her hand to reassure me, to let me know she was always there and would never leave me.'

● Reason 2: The writer never forgets how his efforts to gain the attention of his mother and get her to stay failed and for the first time he felt let down by his parent.

- Evidence 1: '"Mum," I yelled, holding up my latest masterpiece, so certain it would stop her in her tracks, send her running in my direction to scoop me up and take us both to the park. She didn't look back. She kept on walking.'
- Evidence 2: 'Mum was leaving me with a complete stranger; it felt like the ultimate betrayal.'
- Reason 3: It was memorable because the child could not make sense of the situation and did not know when his mother would be returning.
  - Evidence 1: 'I struggled to make sense of what was happening.'
  - Evidence 2: '"Soon." What did that mean? What four-year-old understands the word "soon"?'
- Reason 4: It was memorable because, once the mother has left, the teacher fails to make the child feel special or safe and her attempts to reassure the child are brief and insincere.
  - Evidence 1: '"Mum will be back soon," said the stranger, smiling, but it wasn't a "Mum" smile; it was the same smile she had for all the other crying kids.'
  - Evidence 2: '"Mum will be back soon," she repeated, but already she had an eye on the boy throwing sand at the opposite side of the room.'

Page 44, Analysing a hotel brochure

Comment on how language has been used to convey the impression that this would be a good place for a relaxing break.

In your response, you may have selected and explained the following:

- Engaging opening due to personal pronoun and question to begin, 'Are you looking for the perfect short stay to recharge your batteries?'
- Implies the hotel is easily accessible, 'Only 18 miles outside of Dublin...'
- States opinion as fact, 'the perfect base for a tranquil weekend break', and includes 'tranquil' to suggest that, despite its closeness to the city, it is calm and peaceful.
- Positive adjectives: 'stunning', 'luxurious', 'spacious', 'award-winning', 'breath-taking', 'exotic', 'delicious' and 'spectacular' encourage the reader to form positive expectations of the hotel, its accommodation, its facilities, its grounds and its food.
- '...totally transformed' makes the refurbishment seem impressive.
- Makes it seem like value for money, 'starter, main and dessert for only €20 per person'.
- Gives the impression the guest comes first, '...so you can enjoy a well-deserved lie-in and check out is not until 2.00pm so you can soak up all the hotel has to offer'.
- Implies that this will be an unforgettable experience, 'Create memories you will cherish for a lifetime.'
- Implies that a stay here will allow you to unwind and recharge, physically and mentally, '...your body and mind will thank you for it'.

Page 54, Analysing presentational devices

Your response may identify and explain two of the following presentational devices:

Colour	Use of blue on page 1 links to water theme which is appropriate as the text is about attractions within the Lakelands area.
	Blue and white dominates page 1 and page 2 features green. These are colours associated with nature and outdoors making them appropriate for a text which is about exploring the Fermanagh Lakelands.
	White for titles ensures they stand out and suggest this is a place of untainted beauty.
	Photographs are in colour to make them appealing to the reader.
Layout	Page 1 is dominated by image to capture the attention of a reader.
	The 'swirls' on page 1 look like ripples on water, reminding the reader the lakes are a central attraction.
	The blue and white lines add a modern quality to page 1 to suggest the Lakelands offer visitors an infusion of historic and modern sights and experiences.
	Page 2 features a collection of images at the top of the page with informative text placed below for the reader who wants to find out more.
	The table on page 2 helps the reader locate information easily and quickly.
	On page 1 the title 'Fermanagh Lakelands' is positioned towards the top, suggesting this is a highly regarded location which offers visitors high-quality attractions and experiences.

Images	Page 1's close up shot captures the reader's attention and makes them think this is a place where history comes alive. It will appeal to those with an interest in the past and makes the reader think a visit here can be fun and educational.
	The child is dressed up which will appeal to children who will enjoy the interactive nature of the attractions.
	The adult figure is in historical dress, suggesting visitors will have an opportunity to immerse themselves in the history of the area.
	The adult is assisting the child, reassuring the reader that people and staff in the Lakelands area are welcoming and kind.
	On page 2 there is a collection of 'taster shots' to give the reader an indication of the variety of attractions on offer in the area.
	The different images are placed around the central picture of the castle and the lake to emphasise that a visit to explore the lakes will also offer many additional sights and experiences.
	A mix of old and modern photographs support the idea that this is a place with a rich history to be discovered by visitors.
	Images feature young and old to suggest the area will appeal to people of all ages.
	Images show the area appeals to those who like to relax and soak up scenery, as well as those who enjoy attending large, colourful outdoor events. The reader thinks there is plenty to see and do.
Font	Includes a variety of font styles and sizes with larger font for titles and headings to help the reader navigate the text.
	The font style is sophisticated to suggest this is a place of culture and class.
	The font style is quite modern with the 'H' of 'History' and 'Heritage' and the 'T' of 'Trails' looking more traditional to reinforce the suggestion that the Fermanagh Lakelands offer a mix of modern and traditional attractions.

Unit 4, Section A

For all of the following tasks, use the mark schemes that follow to assess how successful your response is.

- Page 62: Write a personal essay about a place you would like to live.
- Page 66: Write a creative response based on character.
- Page 68: Write a creative response based on setting.
- Page 75: Using what you have learned, answer

either the Personal or Creative Writing task below:
Write a personal essay for the examiner about a time you made a discovery.

OR

Write a creative response for the examiner. Your writing should be based on the image. Give your work a suitable title.

Content

Level 1	Limited development of ideas with simple descriptions and few language techniques.
	Simple awareness of purpose, audience and form.
Level 2	Some successful communication and development of ideas with attempts to use language techniques which are fitting for audience and purpose.
	Sensible organisation of ideas which, in places, might be linked by structural features.
Level 3	Mostly successful communication and development of original ideas and descriptions.
	Uses language techniques with increasing success to gain the interest of the audience.
	Successful organisation of ideas with clear evidence of structural features.
Level 4	Communicates and develops ideas in a way that is original and convincing.
	Successfully uses a variety of language techniques throughout the response to enhance the engagement of the reader.
	Skilful organisation of ideas.
Level 5	Highly confident development of ideas in a style which is highly engaging and successfully hooks and holds the reader's interest.
	Confidently employs a full range of language techniques which are used precisely to make the writing original and compelling.
	Assured organisation of ideas with structural features.

SPG

Level 1	Simple sentence structuring.
	Basic punctuation used with some accuracy.
	Limited vocabulary with some accuracy in spelling of simple words.
Level 2	Straightforward sentence structuring.
	Accurate use of simple punctuation, such as full stops and commas, to achieve straightforward communication.
	Some evidence of vocabulary used to enhance the response with accurate spelling of uncomplicated words.
Level 3	Some variation in sentence structures.
	Accurate use of full stops, commas, question marks and exclamation marks with some evidence of punctuation deliberately used to add impact.
	Attempts to use a wide and varied vocabulary, including some ambitious words.
Level 4	Evidence of deliberate variation in sentence structures to enhance meaning.
	Successfully employs a range of punctuation throughout the response.
	Accurate spelling, with only occasional errors in the use of challenging words.
	Evidence of a precise and varied vocabulary.
Level 5	A full range of sentence structures are used to enhance the overall response.
	Confidently uses a full range of punctuation.
	Virtually all spellings are accurate with only one-off errors which are likely to occur as an attempt to use more ambitious and complex language.
	Evidence of sophisticated vocabulary.

Unit 4, Section B

Pages 81–82, Comparing and contrasting how an atmosphere of tension has been created in two literary texts

In your response, you may have selected and explained the following:

- Text A is written using a first-person perspective which helps create tension by immersing the reader into the situation of the main character and making it feel immediate **whereas Text B** is written using a third-person narrative perspective with tension created through the descriptions of sudden actions and reactions.
- **Both** texts open abruptly and use short sentences to establish tension.
- **Both** texts use repetition to communicate a sense of urgency – 'Screaming and screaming' (A) and 'had to…' (B).
- In Text A two short, dramatic paragraphs emphasise the atmosphere of tension as the narrator states, 'It's my voice', exaggerating his sense of solitude and

the fact he is so tense and panicked that he barely recognised his own voice. Exclamatory sentences reinforce his desperation to locate Amy.

- In **Text A**, the description of setting creates an eerie and tense atmosphere **whereas**, in **Text B**, Brian's reaction to the situation, and his reluctance to touch the dead pilot increase the tension.
- In **Text B**, the tension is maintained as Brian takes control of the plane but we infer he is inexperienced as it states he was 'waiting to see what would happen'. The tension is then momentarily eased once Brian takes control of the plane and it flies, 'normally, smoothly'.
- In **Text A**, the narrator returns to the dyke but this time describes how it has changed. Dramatic verbs such as 'blasted' and a simile, 'as if some careless giant had passed by…'. The strange description of the wood as 'melted' is intriguing and forces the narrator and the reader to speculate.
- In **Text B**, tension escalates again through the use of short sentences and vague language – 'Now to do this thing.' The reader anticipates a dramatic development.

- **Both** texts conclude dramatically and maintain a level of tension. In **Text A**, the verb 'cry' and the description of 'the gaping dark of the cemetery' are foreboding and make the main character seem vulnerable. **Likewise**, in **Text B**, the situation is tense as the plane 'went through another series of stomach-wrenching swoops up and down before he could get it under control'. The longer sentence here reflects Brian's panicked efforts to get the plane under control.
- By the end of **Text A** the reader feels intrigued and concerned for the main character and we speculate his search for Amy will continue to be a tense and challenging one. **Whereas**, in **Text B**, the reader feels that Brian is safe for the minute, but the text up to this point, has shown that his journey to safety is unpredictable and tense. In **both** texts the final fate of the main character remains unknown.

Page 87, 'Generation selfie'

1 In your response, you may have selected and explained the following:
   ○ Engaging title posed as a question with triple verbs and alliteration of 'p' grabbing the reader's attention and inclusive language – 'us' – making the subject seem relevant to the reader.
   ○ Anecdotal opening to immerse the reader into the writer's world to allow us to relate to her concern about her online image.
   ○ Simile – 'why I'm reacting like a celebrity who has just spotted a paparazzo…' is humorous and lets us know she is aware that her reaction is over the top.
   ○ Long sentence to begin paragraph two emphasises her exaggerated reaction.
   ○ Humour is injected as she admits her husband is the 'saner' voice but she confidently asserts that her reaction is 'normal' and confidently states that 'most women I know would react the same way'. She seems to be implying females are more image conscious and obsessed with controlling their online image.
   ○ Words such as 'meticulously police' and 'high-maintenance' make her concern seem unhealthy and obsessive.
   ○ The reader appreciates the confessional tone of the writer as she admits, 'yet I know my good angles, I've perfected a selfie-smile and

I have preferred Instagram filters'. This triple emphasises just how concerned she is with controlling her online image.
   ○ Short sentence, 'And I'm not the only one.' The tone is emphatic, encouraging the reader to agree.
   ○ Final sentence, 'Vanity has exploded on an epic scale', contains hyperbole and the word 'exploded' carries negative connotations, suggesting this is something out of control.

2 In your response, you may have selected and explained the following:
   ○ Writer flashes back to her pre-Instagram days and recalls that 'within weeks' she'd made a new discovery. The reader infers that this obsession developed unexpectedly but very rapidly.
   ○ Humorously she refers to 'the dark arts of the selfie', making it seem sinister and dangerous.
   ○ List of three shows how her selfie obsession took hold of her – 'grinning in a kagoul in an Alpine hut, drinking Guinness in a Belfast bar, waving from a sunlounger in Antigua'. The reader infers that experiences are no longer private.
   ○ Verb choice, 'I've learnt', implies that this is not a simple pleasure but something to be worked at and perfected.
   ○ 'I'm on my way to adopting…' implies that she feels she must change as a consequence of her selfie obsession. The reader recognises the writer's admission that there is nothing natural about her selfies as everything is staged.
   ○ References to well-known female celebrities encourage the reader to see how ordinary people are influenced by others and the selfie obsession has been fuelled by celebrity images.
   ○ Humorous anecdote makes the reader appreciate how extreme the writer's obsession has become, that she will shout at a policeman. Repetition of 'terrifying' makes us view her behaviour in a negative way. The writer is aware of her extreme behaviour but seems powerless to tame it – longer sentences help convey this impression.
   ○ She defines her selfie obsession and need to control her images as 'art direction', which confirms that she can't stop it so she tries to make it sound acceptable rather than stating it for what it is. This is humorous but the serious message is not lost upon the reader.